POLITICAL PROFILES
AL GORE

Political Profiles
Al Gore

Kerrily Sapet

**MORGAN
REYNOLDS**

PUBLISHING

Greensboro, North Carolina

POLITICAL PROFILES

Barack Obama
Hillary Clinton
John McCain
Nancy Pelosi
Al Gore
Rudy Giuliani
Arnold Schwarzenegger

POLITICAL PROFILES: AL GORE

Copyright © 2008 by Kerrily Sapet

Library of Congress Cataloging-in-Publication Data

Sapet, Kerrily, 1972-
   Political profiles : Al Gore / by Kerrily Sapet.
      p. cm.
   Includes bibliographical references and index.
   ISBN-13: 978-1-59935-070-7
   ISBN-10: 1-59935-070-X
   1. Gore, Albert, 1948---Juvenile literature. 2. Vice-Presidents--United States-
-Biography--Juvenile literature. 3. Legislators--United States--Biography--
Juvenile literature. 4. United States. Congress. Senate--Biography--Juvenile
literature. 5. Presidential candidates--United States--Biography--Juvenile lit-
erature. 6. Environmentalists--United States--Biography--Juvenile literature.
I. Title.
   E840.8.G65S27 2007
   973.929092--dc22
   [B]

                                        2007031247

Printed in the United States of America
First Edition

To my father, for sharing his love of history

Contents

Al Gore
(Courtesy of AP Images/Susan Walsh)

one

Tennesse's Son

When he was growing up, Al Gore's life was sharply divided. He spent most summers on his family's farm in the middle of Tennessee. There he swam in Caney Fork River, canoed past the river's rocky banks, and fished. It was not all fun and relaxation, though; he also had to milk cows and help tend to the family's tobacco crops. At night, he slept at his grandmother's house in a feather bed.

Al loved life at the farm, situated in the rolling, wooded hills outside the small town of Carthage. But with the first touch of autumn's chill, he and his family moved back to the politically charged atmosphere of Washington, D.C., where Al's father served in the United States Congress. Suddenly, Al's surroundings changed from lush, relaxing fields to the stone buildings of a strict private boy's school.

This mix of country and city life helped to define Al Gore. He would eventually follow his father into the rough world of politics, but a part of him would always long for the quiet of the farm.

Albert Arnold Gore Jr. was born in Washington, D.C. on March 31, 1948. The birth of a son delighted his parents, Albert and Pauline. Their daughter, ten-year-old Nancy, nicknamed her little brother Bo, but the whole family called him Little Al.

A young Gore sits with his father, Al Gore Sr., and his mother, Pauline. (*Courtesy of AP Images/The Tennessean*)

Al Gore Sr. had been born in Tennessee in 1907, the third of five children. He grew up on a small, poor farm in Possum Hollow, near Nashville, Tennessee. Although the names of the surrounding towns—Defeated, Difficult, Nameless—echoed the isolation and relentless poverty of the area, the Gore family was ambitious.

Al Gore Sr. was determined to make his mark. "There was but one way to go from Possum Hollow—that was up and out," he once said. "You couldn't get out except by going up, and once you got out, you still were pretty far down that pole."

He hauled livestock to market, raised tobacco, sold radios door-to-door, and taught in a one room schoolhouse. The only member of his generation from Possum Hollow to go to college, he attended Murfreesboro State, scraping money together for one semester at a time. After graduation he continued teaching, became a principal, and then a school superintendent. Gore also drove sixty miles to Nashville and back three times a week to attend an evening law school run by the Nashville YMCA.

On these trips he often stopped for coffee at the Andrew Jackson Hotel, where he first met twenty-one-year-old Pauline LaFon, a tall, determined woman. Also from a small Tennessee farming community, Pauline worked at the coffee shop to pay her way through Vanderbilt Law School. During the Depression that gripped the country in the early 1930s, she had watched her father's business fail. Her family had to open their modest home to boarders to make ends meet.

One of six children, Pauline had decided to work her way out of her poor hometown. She would be one of the first two women to earn a law degree from Vanderbilt. Al and Pauline married on May 15, 1937, and soon after, she left her job to raise children and support her husband's career.

A year after the couple married, Gore ran for a vacant congressional seat as a Democrat and won. Pauline was active in her husband's campaign. Socially and politically astute, she volunteered in her husband's congressional office when he went to Washington.

Representative Gore made headlines when he became the first congressman to enlist at the beginning of World War II, although he was exempt from the military draft. Two years later, after his tour, he returned to Congress.

In 1952, after serving in the House of Representatives for fourteen years, Al Gore Sr. ran for a seat in the Senate. In the race he challenged popular and powerful veteran senator Kenneth D. McKellar. Known as "Old Formidable," McKellar had represented Tennessee for thirty-five years.

Most political observers thought Gore didn't stand a chance. But Al and Pauline ran an enthusiastic campaign. Gore and his supporters bragged about his Tennessee background as a poor farm boy who had worked his way up. "The twang of Smith County is still in his voice and the steel of hard work is still in his muscles," they said.

Their four-year-old son, Al Jr., helped too, absorbing valuable campaign lessons, even at his young age. Once when he and a friend went out for ice cream they saw a policeman. "I'll ask him to vote for my daddy," he said. Al's friend suggested the officer might vote for him anyway. "No," he responded. "You've got to ask 'em."

Al Gore Sr. defeated McKellar, and the Gores moved into the Fairfax Hotel, billed as Washington's Family Hotel. Congressmen and diplomats filled the floors of the exclusive

The Fairfax Hotel became Gore's home in Washington, D.C., during his father's tenure as a senator. *(Library of Congress)*

hotel and the air was thick with politics. On warm summer evenings, adults congregated by the hotel's rooftop gardens to catch a cool breeze and to hear the latest political gossip.

To dark-haired, freckled Al Jr., the hotel was a fancy playground. He and his friends clambered up the metal staircase to the roof, where they played Frisbee and dropped water balloons on limousines parked below. They also tied plastic figures to spools of thread and dangled the toys down over the hotel's front entrance, hoping to bop guests on the head. At other times, the young boy floated his toy submarine in the Senate pool.

The Gores were part of the Washington political elite. The family visited Richard Nixon when he was vice president under Dwight Eisenhower. Sometimes he answered the phone to hear the White House phone operator asking for his father to please call President Kennedy.

When he was old enough, Al Jr. attended St. Albans, a private boy's school. Founded in the nineteenth century, St. Albans originally served as a school for choirboys at Washington's National Cathedral. It had been converted into a boarding school.

The campus's towering Gothic buildings echoed the school's strict standards of discipline. The headmaster, Canon Charles Martin, imposed strong academic, moral, and social values. He walked around campus with his bulldog, Mark Anthony, greeting students from behind with a firm grip on the back of the neck. Martin instructed boarders' parents to write letters dispensing advice such as, "Love—not the kind that is sentimental and soft, but real love with the iron of justice and right in it—is the basis of all good relationships."

Although he lived in a busy, crowded city most of the year, some people remember Little Al as a lonely child. His father worked long hours and frequently traveled, often back to Tennessee, and his mother was one of Washington's busiest political wives. She gave speeches, raised money, and ran a training program to familiarize other politician's wives with important issues and campaign techniques.

Several nights a week Al ate with his cousins, Jamie, Mark, and Celeste, who lived in the townhouse next door. The Gores also hired two women from Tennessee to help while the family was in Washington. On long weekends, holidays, and summer breaks, Al stayed in Carthage with Will and Alota Thompson, who oversaw the Gores' farm. Al went from his ritzy Washington hotel to their small home with no electricity or running water.

Most of Gore's young life was divided between his homes in Tennessee and Washington, D.C. Gore stands with his parents and his sister, Nancy (far left), as they prepare to leave their Tennessee home.
(Courtesy of AP Images/Joe Rudis/The Tennessean)

Even in Tennessee, Al's father had demanding standards. At twelve years old, Al's day began at dawn with fifty push-ups followed by farm chores. At the end of the exhausting day he sometimes fell asleep in his clothes. Will Thompson would carry him up to bed. In addition to his chores, Al also had extra school work. "Al's father would just work the dickens out of him," said Al's cousin Mark. "Up at dawn, very serious work for a kid."

Al eventually found friends in Tennessee. On warm summer nights, he and the Thompsons' son Gordon, nicknamed "Goat," set up a tent in the yard and stayed up late playing cards and checkers. To cool off they swam in the river or the murky water of the cow trough. Up in the barn's hayloft, Al and his friends built tunnels and fortresses in the sweet-smelling hay. They called themselves the Tootsie Roll Gang because one day a truck hauling Tootsie Rolls overturned on the highway, spilling candy all over the road. Stuffing as much as they could into their pockets, the boys took the candy to a secret hiding place in the woods. There they sat, peeling off the candy's brown and white wrappers, eating Tootsie Rolls until they could eat no more.

One summer on the farm, when Al was thirteen, he met Donna Armistead. They dated for three years, seeing movies and frequenting a local diner for cheeseburgers and banana milkshakes. Together they water-skied on the nearby lake, and Al learned how to balance on the outboard motor on his head.

Whether in Carthage or in Washington, Al impressed people. He was intelligent, polite, and handsome. At St. Albans, he spent two years as the class treasurer and excelled at basketball, football, and track. Senior year he was named captain of the football team. An avid record collector, Al went to the first concert the Beatles gave in the United States. Even with all of his activities, Al maintained top grades.

Al's sister Nancy made it to as many of her brother's activities as she could. Defiant and rambunctious, Nancy was the opposite of her quiet, eager-to-please brother, but the two were close, despite their age difference.

At Al's senior prom, in May of 1965, he met Mary Elizabeth Aitcheson, a pretty blue-eyed girl with long blonde hair. Her mother had nicknamed her "Tipper," after a popular song called "Ti-Pi-Tin." Although Tipper was someone else's prom date, Al called her the next day and asked her out.

Tipper, a junior at St. Agnes Episcopal School for Girls, was vivacious and friendly. She enjoyed music and played drums for a rock group called "The Wildcats." She and her mother lived in Arlington, Virginia, in her grandmother's house. Tipper's parents had divorced when she was two years old. Although she saw her father weekly, Tipper had a somewhat lonely childhood; she often had to help her mother battle depression.

Al and Tipper began dating steadily. After he graduated from St. Albans, Al was accepted at Harvard University in Cambridge, Massachusetts. The summer before his freshman year he invited Tipper to the family farm. Just as Al had hoped, Tipper and his parents liked each other.

In the fall of 1965, Al left for college in Massachusetts. Tipper, who was a year behind him in school, stayed; they continued their relationship through letters.

two

Harvard, War, and Love

When Al Gore arrived at Harvard, he entered an environment much different than St. Albans. At St. Albans the high-school students had spent their days nestled in a cocoon of studying, listening to the music of Bob Dylan. They had been stunned by President Kennedy's assassination on November 22, 1963, as was the entire country, but little else broke through the wall that separated St. Albans from the world.

At Harvard, Gore found a group of students who thrived on challenging authority and questioning the government. College students had always pushed against authority, but something was different in the last half of the 1960s. The Vietnam War cast an increasingly bigger shadow over the entire country, especially on college campuses where students passionately protested against what they saw as an unjust and brutal war.

It took a while for the new, more serious world of college to make an impression on Gore. One of his first new

Harvard students hold hands and march around University Hall during a protest against the Vietnam War. *(Courtesy of AP Images)*

friends was his dorm mate Tommy Lee Jones, the future Academy Award winning actor.

Gore worked hard his freshman year, getting decent grades. He was elected class president, but did not intend to follow his father into politics. He wanted a career in writing, although he struggled with poetry and Russian literature.

Although Gore was known to be serious, he achieved some notoriety for riding his motorcycle back to school after winter break in Washington. He arrived nearly frozen.

In 1966, after Gore's first year at Harvard, Tipper graduated from high school. She decided to attend Garland Junior College in Boston and would later transfer to Boston University to study child psychology. Later that summer, Al's sister Nancy married. In a small ceremony at the family's farmhouse, she wed Frank Hunger, a country lawyer and former Air Force pilot.

Gore's academic focus sharpened during his junior year when he took a course about the American presidency. The professor, Richard Neustadt, had served as an adviser to presidents Truman and Kennedy. He sprinkled his lectures with rich case studies illustrating presidential decision making. The fresh, challenging material intrigued Gore and he asked Neustadt shrewd questions. He decided to switch his major to government.

Harvard professor and oceanographer Roger Revelle also influenced Gore. In the 1930s, Revelle had collected mud samples from the ocean floor and analyzed their carbon dioxide content. His studies pointed to escalating levels of carbon dioxide in the earth's atmosphere. This rise in carbon dioxide traps the sun's heat and increases the earth's temperature, creating what is called the greenhouse gas effect. Revelle's lectures sparked a lifelong interest in the environment for Gore.

At the time, though, there were more pressing matters. By 1967, the United States was deeply entrenched in the war in Vietnam. Located in Southeast Asia, Vietnam was a divided country. North Vietnam was communist and aligned with the Soviet Union; South Vietnam had rejected Communism and depended on the United States for its survival. As the conflict between the north and the south escalated, the United States poured massive amounts of political, military, and economic aid into South Vietnam.

After President Kennedy was assassinated, the new president, Lyndon Johnson, escalated American's involvement. Then, in August 1964, after an attack on American ships off

By 1967, America was heavily involved in the Vietnam War. *(Courtesy of the National Archives and Records Administration)*

the coast of Vietnam in the Gulf of Tonkin, Congress gave President Johnson permission to do whatever he thought necessary to win the war for South Vietnam. By March of 1965, tens of thousands of U.S. troops were fighting and dying in Vietnam.

Before long, however, many Americans began to question the U.S. participation in the war. What were the objectives, they asked, and when would we know that victory had been achieved. There had been treaties and agreements between the two sides before, but they had been broken. The U.S. was restrained from invading North Vietnam and removing the Communist government because of its alliance with the Soviet Union, which had thousands of nuclear missiles pointed toward the U.S. and our European allies. As the situation began to seem more and more hopeless, opposition to the war became more determined.

Few young men volunteered to join the military, and the U.S. government began a draft, requiring men between the ages of eighteen and twenty-five to register and face the possibility of being forced to fight in Vietnam. As the war progressed, and thousands of young Americans were killed and injured in combat, opposition to the war flared to a white heat. By the fall of 1967, ending U.S. involvement in the Vietnam War became the dominant issue on college campuses.

While undergraduate students at universities were still exempt from the draft, President Johnson ended deferments, or exemptions, for most graduate students. Soon he doubled the monthly draft call to 35,000 men each month. "In September [of 1967] the new climate was obvious," wrote Steven Kelman, a Harvard antiwar activist. "A peaceful campus, only marginally concerned with Vietnam, suddenly became desperate. We felt boxed in. We were like the man about to go into the gas chamber, with no way out and walls slowly but inexorably closing around us."

Thousands of young men had planned to attend graduate programs, waiting out the draft until the end of the war or until they turned twenty-six years old, the age of ineligibility. Draft exemptions were maintained for graduate students in divinity and education, and these programs suddenly surged in popularity. Other desperate young men starved themselves so they would fall under the 120-pound cutoff during their draft physicals. Medical students helped undergraduates find medically disqualifying conditions, such as migraines and bad backs. Others fled to Canada and other countries that provided shelter to those seeking to avoid being sent to Vietnam.

In October of 1967, hundreds of men burned or returned their draft cards to the Justice Department. Lewis Hershey, the Selective Services Director, ordered anyone destroying or returning their draft card to be immediately classified 1-A—draft eligible.

The protests extended beyond the military. At Harvard, students confined a recruiter from DOW chemical company for five hours because the company manufactured napalm, a thickener used to create a sticky explosive gel used in flame-throwers and bombs that produced large amounts of carbon monoxide that caused suffocation. American troops often used napalm to clear helicopter landings in Vietnam, wiping out vegetation and, sometimes, killing civilians.

Despite Al Gore's opposition to the war, he didn't become actively involved in the antiwar movement. He preferred to work through more official channels. In 1968, he helped his father write a speech supporting Eugene McCarthy, a vocal opponent of the war, who was running for the Democratic Party's presidential nominee. That year Hubert Humphrey, Johnson's vice president, won the nomination, despite his association with Johnson's unpopular policies in Vietnam. Republican Richard Nixon defeated Humphrey in the election and continued the U.S. involvement in the Vietnam War.

Gore began his senior year in the midst of this historic turmoil. For his senior thesis he examined the effect of tele-vision on politicians. Still a relatively new medium in 1968, the flickering images on nightly television news reports brought the war's carnage into living rooms. For the first time, Americans had almost instant access to the brutality of war, and this began to have a decisive affect on politicians' behavior, as well as people's attitudes. "Ours was the class that looked at television every night and saw body counts," said Michael Kapitan, Gore's dorm mate. "The war colored our entire college experience."

Gore proposed to Tipper before he graduated in June of 1969. They agreed to marry when she graduated from college the following spring. The year ahead would be an uncertain one. After graduation he was eligible for the draft. As the son of an influential senator he could pull strings to avoid the draft. "If you have the dough, you don't have to go," went one saying of the time. But Gore knew that decision could have serious repercussions for others. "In Carthage, Tennessee, it was no secret who was on the draft board, what the rough quota was each month," Gore said later. "And if you didn't go, it was no secret that one of your friends would have to go in your place."

The war made its mark on Carthage in July of 1969, when the *Carthage Courier* announced that local nineteen-year-old Shannon Wills had been killed in Vietnam. "His death could be accepted with more grace if our country were fighting for its life, or if we were threatened with invasion, or if we were threatened with extinction as we were in World War Two," read the newspaper's editorial. "The question all of us ask, and for which we have found no answer is, why?"

More and more Americans were asking this same question, including Al Gore. Moral, emotional, and social questions about serving in Vietnam plagued him. There was also another factor he had to consider, however. If he avoided the draft, Gore could damage his father's career.

An outspoken opponent of the war, Al Gore Sr. believed President Nixon was purposely misleading the country about the extent of U.S. involvement in Vietnam. His views hurt him politically in conservative Tennessee and angered the president. If Al avoided service in Vietnam, it could be the final blow to his father's career.

Family and regional traditions also were at stake. Al Gore Sr. had served in World War II, and Tennessee's nickname was the Volunteer State. After weighing all of the factors, Gore decided to face military service without any special favors, although he disagreed with American involvement in Vietnam. In August of 1969, he enlisted in the Army.

Gore opted for a two-year commitment, the same as draftees. As part of the Army's sales pitch, men who enlisted for three years had their choice of select jobs. "Make your choice now. Join, or we'll make the choice for you," read one ad.

Gore (back row, second from right) stands with a group of fellow soldiers in this 1971 photo. *(Courtesy of AP Images)*

Gore took his chances so he could limit his enlistment to two years. Most servicemen who voluntarily enlisted and were able to quickly learn new skills weren't assigned to combat. Gore was eventually made an information specialist, writing press releases and articles for military newspapers.

In October of 1969, he reported for basic training at Fort Rucker, an aviation school in southern Alabama where men were trained to pilot helicopters and to be door gunners. Before they were shipped out to Vietnam for combat duty, lawyers helped the young men draw up their wills. During his basic training, Gore drilled and learned hand-to-hand combat skills.

Protests against the war continued. On Moratorium Day, October 15, 1969, millions of Americans stayed home from jobs and classes to protest the war. One month later at least 500,000 people marched in Washington in what was dubbed the March Against Death. The following spring, when it was revealed that President Nixon had been secretly bombing in Cambodia, a neighboring country, a rash of violent protests broke out. At Kent State University in Ohio, National Guardsmen fired into a crowd of student demonstrators, killing four. The event horrified the country.

Two weeks later, Gore took a quick leave. Tipper had graduated from Boston University with a degree in child psychology, and on May 19, 1970, the two married at the National Cathedral in Washington. Gore wore his formal dress blues Army uniform and Tipper wore a white lace gown and carried a bouquet of orchids. The newlyweds walked down the aisle to the Beatles tune "All You Need is Love" played on the organ.

In 1970, Gore and Tipper married at the National Cathedral in Washington. In this photo, the newlyweds celebrate with Gore's parents. *(Courtesy of AP Images)*

After a honeymoon in Hawaii, the couple moved to Daleville, Alabama, a few miles from Fort Rucker. They went from fairytale wedding attended by some of the nation's most powerful people to an Army base trailer park. Determined to live on Gore's military pay, Tipper was horrified after opening the refrigerator door in one potential home. At first she thought the refrigerator's interior was painted black, then realized the black was wriggling cockroaches.

In November of 1970, Al Gore Sr. narrowly lost his Senate seat, ending a long and distinguished career. His challenger, William Brock, had run a fierce campaign that accused him of being soft on Communism because of his antiwar stance. Gore had also antagonized many white voters by supporting

President Johnson's racial integration policies. After thirty-two years of public service, Al Gore Sr. was a private citizen.

In Alabama, his son despaired at the direction the country was taking. Over the last decade, President Kennedy and civil rights leader Martin Luther King Jr. had fallen victim to assassins. Now Gore's father, an intelligent, dedicated public servant, had been defeated. His interest in politics dissipated, and he told friends he would find another way to make a difference.

But his plans for the future would have to wait. At the end of 1970, Gore received orders to ship out to Vietnam. After a bleak Christmas, he left his new wife, his family, and his friends behind. He was bound for a war he loathed.

three
Serving His Country

On January 8, 1971, after a thirteen-hour flight across the Pacific Ocean, Al Gore stepped onto the airstrip tarmac in Bien Hoa, South Vietnam. A blast of hot smoky air hit him. Fighters, bombers, and helicopters took off at the air base twenty-four hours a day. He watched as ragged, dusty soldiers passed him, headed home to the United States. Nearby, on the crowded streets of Saigon, local women hawked marijuana cigarettes and other black-market goods.

Gore began his work as an Army journalist, assigned to the 20th Engineer Brigade. The headquarters handled personnel, press, and communications. His job was to interview soldiers after they had seen action. Some of the servicemen worried that Gore, as a senator's son, would get preferred treatment. "A lot of guys made up their minds that they weren't going to be too happy about someone who was getting the lobster treatment when everyone else was getting the fishbones," said

Alan Leo, a photographer in the press office where Gore worked.

Most of them soon realized Gore wanted no such treatment. Like everyone else, he carried out orders, borrowed cigarettes, and mocked superior officers who annoyed him.

When Gore arrived in Vietnam the war was in its final throes. President Nixon was withdrawing troops at the rate of 12,000 to 15,000 a month. The pullouts actually lowered morale even more because the men knew they were biding their time in a lost cause. They did whatever they could to survive physically and mentally, even, in some extreme cases, killing officers who ordered them into combat. No one wanted to die waiting to leave a lost war. "The men themselves are fed up with the war and the draft, questioning orders, deserting, subverting, smoking marijuana, shooting heroin, stealing from their buddies," said B. Drummond Ayres Jr., a *New York Times* correspondent.

Gore is on duty as an Army journalist in Vietnam in this 1971 photo. *(Courtesy of AP Images)*

Although he never saw combat, Gore witnessed and heard terrible stories that would haunt him. He and photographer Bob Delabar covered a medal ceremony honoring Army helicopter pilot Hugh Thompson. According to the citation, Thompson and his men, under heavy enemy fire, had rescued South Vietnamese civilians in a small village on the My Lai Peninsula.

A few months later, the world learned the full story about the rescue. The South Vietnamese refugees were not escaping the Communists. They were fleeing troops under the command of Lieutenant William Calley, who had killed hundreds of civilians. Thompson had set his helicopter down and ordered his men to open fire on Calley's troops if they continued to harm anyone. Thompson had won his medal protecting civilians from American troops.

On May 22, 1971, Gore left Vietnam. By the time the last American combat troops left Vietnam on April 30, 1975, an estimated 58,226 American soldiers, one million Vietnamese soldiers, and four million Vietnamese civilians had been killed. After one year and nine months in uniform, Gore was one of the lucky ones. Shaken and changed, he returned home to his wife, who had waited anxiously for him to return safely.

After his return home, he and Tipper stayed at the Gore family farm in Carthage, where he took long, late-night walks. Searching for some quiet time, the couple eventually embarked on a cross-country camping trip. They loaded up their car with a tent, two sleeping bags, a cooler, a camera, and a backpack of books and traveled through Michigan, Wisconsin, and Minnesota, then headed west to California, meeting with friends along the way. They camped in National

After returning from Vietnam, Gore and Tipper set out on a cross-country camping trip, during which they saw the towering redwood trees of California.

Parks and forests, seeing the open landscape of Yellowstone and marveling at California's giant redwood trees. When they returned to Tennessee, Gore sought to reconcile his experiences in Vietnam by attending Vanderbilt Divinity School in Nashville. He also looked for a job.

During Gore's service he had occasionally sent Tipper and his father copies of the articles he wrote for military newspapers. They shared them with John Seigenthaler, editor of the *Tennessean,* a Nashville-based newspaper. Gore's writing had impressed Siegenthaler, and the editor invited Gore for a job interview. City editor Frank Ritter asked his favorite question during the interview—"What would [you] do if an editor ordered [you] to write a story [you] knew to be untrue?"

"I can't imagine that an editor would ever ask a reporter to do that," Gore answered. "It would be unprofessional. But if it happened, I would resign before I violated my con- science." It was "the best answer I've ever gotten," said Ritter. He gave Gore the job.

In 1971, Gore and Tipper moved to Nashville and he began working as a night-shift reporter. He hammered away at his electric typewriter and penciled in changes before handing pages over to the editor. At first, Gore wanted nothing to do with politics. He refused to write about it and declined his parent's invitations to political functions. But Gore couldn't shake his Washington upbringing. At Harvard, Professor Neustadt's lectures had once sparked interest in him, now

Gore consults with photographer Bill Preston (left) while working as a reporter for the *Tennessean*. *(Courtesy of AP Images/The Tennessean, Billy Easley)*

local politics did the same. He began to cover Nashville politics and developed a reputation for being curious and tenacious.

Unsure of whether journalism should be his career, Gore dabbled with a land-development company and experimented as a farmer, raising livestock and growing tobacco. He and Tipper bought a house in Nashville and a farm in Carthage across the river from his childhood farmhouse.

Tipper too was busy. After taking a photography course she got a part-time job as a photographer at the *Tennessean*. She also began graduate work to earn a master's degree in child psychology. On August 6, 1973, the Gores' first child, a daughter, was born. They named her Karenna.

That same year Gore uncovered a story about a councilman soliciting bribes from a local developer. His story and tape recordings of the councilman's conversation helped bring the man to trial. But he was shocked when the judge ruled the tapes couldn't be used as evidence, and he became more interested in the workings of the legal system.

On August 28, 1974, Gore dropped his divinity coursework and entered Vanderbilt Law School. Like his father and mother before him, he saw law school as a path to the future. During his time in law school, Gore studied political and social policy issues. He considered the idea that as a politician he could gather facts, the aspect he enjoyed most about reporting. If he entered politics he might be able to find a way to act on that information.

In February of 1976, John Seigenthaler told Gore that longtime Tennessee congressman Joe Evins planned to retire. Evins held the same seat Gore's father had held more than thirty years before. Although Gore said he hadn't thought seriously about entering politics, when he learned of the opportunity he called Tipper and announced he was going to run for Congress. "It just came home to me that if I was ever going to do it [run for office], now was the time," Gore said. "Not ten years from now. Not one week from now. Now."

His parents were thrilled, although he wouldn't be able to finish law school. Al Gore Sr. said he was ready to give speeches to get his boy elected. His son declined the offer, however, wanting to win this race himself, and not because of his father's political legacy. The former congressman respected his son's decision.

In the winter of 1976, Al Gore Jr. gave his first political speech. At the county courthouse in Carthage he announced his candidacy for the U.S. House of Representatives. He was so nervous he threw up before the speech.

With the help of his family, Gore ran a homespun campaign, using their farmhouse as headquarters. Their living room was crammed with desks for volunteers and leaflets were everywhere. Gore visited radio stations, newspapers, and every local "meat-and-three," or diners serving specials of a meat and three side dishes.

Even though Gore had watched his parents for years, he was an awkward campaigner, often stiff and nervous giving speeches. He also got carsick trying to read briefing papers between towns on winding country roads. He spent day after day fighting queasiness until his body adjusted. Both he and Tipper found the campaign to be difficult. Tipper called it agony to approach strangers and ask them to vote for her husband. "If I have to go to another tea, I think I'll explode," she told a friend who worked at the newspaper.

Gore pressed on determinedly, spreading his message. He planned to increase taxes for the wealthy, create more job opportunities, and cut defense spending. He visited places two and three times, even when people stomped on his fly-ers, expressing their animosity toward his father.

Gore's main opponent in the race to become the Democratic Party's nominee for the November election was Stanley Rogers. Rogers had more money but campaigned by mak-ing announcements from courthouse steps. Gore rolled up his sleeves and walked into barns and fields to reach peo-ple. He clambered up a telephone pole to talk to a lineman and climbed through a barbed wire fence to meet a farmer on a tractor.

On the night of the primary, Gore paced while watching the news, while his staff subsisted on potato chips and soft drinks. Rogers, who was still the favorite, chartered a heli-copter to fly to Nashville for his victory speech. Then voter returns from two counties bumped Gore to a 2,000 vote lead. He had narrowly edged out Rogers, who called a few min-utes later to congratulate him.

"My family and I know the bitterness of defeat," Gore said in his victory speech. "I have a family that teaches you what public service is all about . . . I consider the office of congressman a sacred trust."

In November 1976, Gore easily defeated an independent candidate, becoming a U.S. representative from Tennessee. After the election, he, Tipper, and their toddler Karenna, moved to Arlington, Virginia, settling into the house Tipper's grandparents had built.

Gore had served his country during the Vietnam War. Now he prepared to serve his country as a congressman. He had followed in his father's footsteps but had taken his own path back to Washington.

four
Making a Difference

On January 4, 1977, Al Gore Jr., twenty-eight, was sworn in as a member of the 95th Congress. As he began his career, he carefully considered his father's strengths and weaknesses as a congressman. Al Gore Sr. had toiled tirelessly behind the scenes, often without receiving public recognition for his hard work. His constituents often did not know how much he had accomplished in their interest. His son intended to be more visible.

Gore made it a priority to stay in touch with his constituents. He set up a punishing schedule, holding one hundred town meetings across Tennessee each year. Whether he met with three people in a country store, or a few hundred at an elementary school, he took his time and listened, hoping to learn what issues were important to the people he was representing.

The next years were busy ones, both personally and professionally. In June of 1977, Gore and Tipper's second daughter,

Kristin, was born. A year later Gore ran unopposed to win a second term. In January 1979, the Gores' third daughter was born. They named her Sarah.

Though moderate on many issues, Gore had progressive positions on volatile issues, such as crime, racial tensions, and poverty. Although a child of Tennessee tobacco farmers, he worked to toughen warning labels on tobacco products. He also joined the Vietnam Veterans caucus. He thought the veterans' physical and psychological needs were largely ignored. Benefit checks often arrived late, and their claims

Gore speaking at a Congressional hearing in 1979 *(Courtesy of AP Images/ John Duricka)*

During his time as a congressman and senator, Gore would often play basketball. *(Courtesy of AP Images/Lennox McLendon)*

for illnesses related to exposure to Agent Orange and other chemicals used in the jungles of Vietnam were too often rejected without investigation. The caucus aimed to offer the veterans the assistance their country owed them.

Gore worked hard, even attempting to type out responses to all of his letters from constituents himself. On weekends he made marathon dashes across Tennessee, sometimes holding as many as six meetings in thirty-six hours. When he did relax, he played basketball with other congressman, ate dinner at Chinese restaurants with his aides, and went to staff parties.

In 1980, his constituents resoundingly reelected Gore for a third term in office. That same year he helped to pass the Superfund law, which provided federal funding for cleaning up hazardous chemical dump sites. For the next five years the Superfund provided $1.6 billion, improving four hundred of the worst toxic waste problems.

On October 19, 1982, the couple's fourth and last child, a son, was born. They named him Albert III. Just one month later Gore was reelected for a fourth term in office. Their lives were rich, full, and busy.

In January of 1983, Howard Baker, a Republican senator from Tennessee, decided not to seek reelection. Gore immediately announced his Senate candidacy. But 1983 was a year of personal tragedy. His sister Nancy was diagnosed with lung cancer. She had smoked cigarettes since she was thirteen, long before the link between tobacco and lung cancer was established. On the evening of July 11, Gore held his sister's hand as she passed away.

A devastated Gore returned to his Senate campaign. Despite his grief, he threw himself into the race, doggedly working to take his platform issues across the state. The future worried Gore, as he considered the effects of greenhouse gases on the earth's atmosphere and the disastrous environmental consequences of a nuclear war. He focused on environmental issues, such as funding wastewater treatment projects and reauthorizing the Clean Air Act.

Gore emerged victorious from a Senate campaign race against two other opponents in 1984. On January 2, 1985, he was sworn in to the Senate to represent Tennessee. At thirty-six, he was one of the youngest senators.

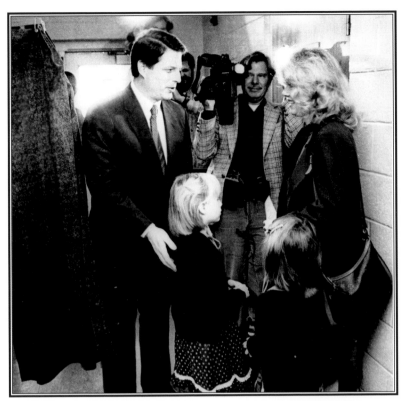

Gore steps out of a polling booth after casting a vote during his 1984 Senate campaign. At right is his wife Tipper and two of their daughters, Kristin and Sarah. *(Courtesy of AP Images/Mark Humphrey)*

That summer Gore gave a speech to a group of female students in Tennessee. He discussed the nuclear arms race raging between the United States and the Soviet Union. During the Cold War the Soviet Union and the United States attempted to build up more nuclear weapons than the other, to be prepared if the other began a nuclear war. Nearly every one of the students said they believed a nuclear war would occur in their lifetime.

The meeting shook Gore. After returning to Washington he began to research the arms race, consulting with experts, such as Leon Fuerth, who sat on the House committee that oversaw arms control issues. From the winter of 1981 to the spring of 1982, Gore and Fuerth met once a week, sometimes for four or five hours at a time. Gradually, he became an expert on nuclear issues.

There were two dominate points of view about the arms race. One side wanted a full-scale military buildup; the other wanted the buildup to stop. More precisely, the administration of President Ronald Reagan wanted to replace aging missiles, which had three nuclear warheads, with the MX missile, which had ten. Critics argued that the MX was not designed to deter a nuclear war, as its supporters said, but was intended to be more capable of launching a successful first strike.

A ten-warhead MX missile
(Courtesy of the U.S. Air Force)

Gore believed there was a middle ground between the two polar positions. In March of 1982 he proposed that the United States and the Soviet Union freeze development of any new weaponry and convert their multiple warhead missiles to single warheads. Russian officials considered Gore's proposal a promising basis for negotiation, but the Reagan administration refused.

Although Gore was not able to stop the buildup, he emerged from the experience wiser and with a new public image as a senator not afraid to tackle controversial issues. He had also shown that he could understand highly technological information. Using this ability, he sponsored the Supercomputer Network Study to explore how to link the nation's supercomputers.

Gore also helped investigate the 1986 explosion of the space shuttle *Challenger*. Thousands of children had crowded into school classrooms around televisions to witness the shuttle's launch, as it carried a teacher, the first civilian to ever be sent into space. Students and adults were horrified when the shuttle exploded. Gore's research helped reveal that the National Aeronautics and Space Administration, NASA, had decreased its quality control staff in the years leading up to the disaster.

In 1986, Gore helped investigate the explosion of the space shuttle *Challenger*. *(Courtesy of NASA)*

Nancy's death spurred Gore to increase his efforts to warn people, especially young people, away from tobacco. "Tomorrow morning another thirteen-year-old girl will start smoking," he said. "Three thousand young people in America will start smoking tomorrow. One thousand of them will die a death not unlike my sister . . . until I draw my last breath, I will pour my heart and my soul into the cause of protecting our children from the dangers of smoking."

Tipper was also busy during these years. She earned her masters degree in psychology and volunteered for several children's organizations. In 1984, after hearing the lyrics from one of her daughter Karenna's records, she started to research popular songs and discovered that many, in her opinion, glorified violence. Believing parents needed help protecting their children from dangerous messages, she wrote the bestselling book *Raising PG Kids in an X-Rated Society.* In 1984, she also started the Parents Music Resource Center, or PMRC, to inform parents about sexual and violent language in popular music. The PMRC proposed voluntary warning labels for records with explicit content. Many record companies began to label their music, but others decried Tipper's actions as censorship. Musician Frank Zappa called her a "cultural terrorist."

Tipper had taken up a highly controversial, even explosive, issue. Musicians began writing songs with scalding, humiliating lyrics about her. She eventually backed off the issue, focusing on less contentious problems, such mental health.

Despite the criticism of PMRC, and his conflict with the popular President Reagan over nuclear weapons, Gore remained widely popular in Tennessee. Although he was not yet forty, influential Democrats and journalists began to mention him as a potential presidential candidate in 1988. President Ronald Reagan was retiring and Vice President George H. W. Bush was the likely Republican candidate.

Despite the talk, few thought Gore would actually enter the race. He was obviously highly intelligent and a talented politician, but they thought his youth, and the fact that he was still largely unknown outside of his home state, meant he would wait to run.

Then, in the spring of 1987, an alliance of forty-five Democrats, called IMPAC 88, offered Gore their support and financial backing if he ran for president. At the same time, several well-known Republicans announced they wouldn't run against Bush. With the field suddenly narrowed, Gore decided to throw his hat into the ring.

On June 29, 1987, Gore declared his candidacy on a blazing, sunny day on the steps of the courthouse in Carthage, Tennessee.

"I know exactly what needs to be done," Gore said, "and I am impatient to do it."

Al Gore Jr. now had to convince voters he should be the next President of the United States.

five

Hope and Heartache

*F*om the start, Gore's presidential campaign encountered problems. Democratic contenders, all better known than Gore, crowded the field. He faced
Massachusetts governor Michael Dukakis, Missouri representative Richard Gephardt, Colorado senator Gary Hart,
and civil rights leader Jesse Jackson, all better known and
more experienced.

Another problem came from Tipper's involvement with the
PMRC. She was accused of advocating censorship. Wealthy
people in California, particularly Hollywood, who typically
make big contributions to candidates, were hostile. Gore's
political advisers warned Tipper's work could seriously under-
cut his success with younger voters, who were typically his
biggest supporters. When asked to contribute to his campaign, Democrat Peggy Kerr responded, "Should the senator get a divorce, please let me know, and I will cheerfully
consider a campaign donation."

Gore was one of many Democratic presidential candidates vying for election in 1988. From left are: Joseph Biden, Michael Dukakis, Jesse Jackson, Bruce Babbit, Gore, Richard Gephardt, and Paul Simon. *(Courtesy of AP Images/Charles Tasnadi)*

Each Democratic candidate struggled to rise to the top. Gore billed himself as liberal on domestic issues, but conservative on foreign policy. In debates he skewered his opponents. Gephardt was accused of constantly reversing his opinions. Dukakis didn't "have a single day of foreign-policy experience" and Jackson didn't have "a single day of experience in government at any level."

Gore's campaign often seemed unfocused. When he announced his candidacy, his long speech outlined several issue, but he had difficulty honing them into a clear, compelling message. One rambling note gave equal importance to nuclear arms control, saving the environment, and landing men on Mars by the year 2000. This diffuse message confused voters.

Trying to overcome fears about his young age, Gore wore a uniform of conservative blue suits and red ties, despite the different ties Tipper packed in his luggage. On chartered planes he sang and amused aides with stories about hypnotizing chickens, but this spontaneous, humorous side was rarely seen in public.

Gore fielded easy questions from local television reporters, such as his favorite color and ice cream flavor, but after Senator Gary Hart had to drop his candidacy because of an extramarital affair, the public, and the journalists, began to scrutinize the candidates' personal lives. The *New York Times* sent a list of questions to each candidate, requesting birth and marriage certificates, as well as information about close friends, medical records, and legal issues. Gore answered the questions he was comfortable with and admitted that he had smoked marijuana while he was in Vietnam.

Despite his honesty, the reviews of Gore as a candidate were mixed. He was praised for his grasp of complicated issues, but criticized for being a lousy campaigner. To worsen matters, money problems plagued the campaign. Only half of IMPAC 88's members delivered the money they had committed to raise.

Gore's family and friends supported him, but the presidential campaign caused tension. Tipper devoted as much time as she could while tending to their four small children. Gore's father campaigned vigorously, planning to tackle forty-eight states. His mother encouraged him too. "Smile, Relax, Attack," read a note she handed him before a debate.

Gore's parents had strict advice for their son and his entire staff. Aides learned to tread carefully around Gore's parents, calling them "Senator Sir and Senator Ma'am." With so many family members involved, questions passed slowly through the family chain of decision making and answers were often inconsistent.

On March 8, 1988, "Super Tuesday," twenty states held their primaries. Democrats and Republicans voted for a candidate to become their party's presidential nominee. It was the big showdown in the race as each party chose its final candidate to run for president in the general election.

Gore earned the most delegate votes in six states, but Governor Dukakis won the most overall. Some candidates dropped out after Super Tuesday, but Gore kept running. Before the New York primary, Gore asked for New York City mayor Ed Koch's support. While campaigning for Gore, Koch made many controversial remarks that offended African Americans and Jewish people, and Gore did poorly in the primary.

After he lost in New York, Gore ended his presidential run. Michael Dukakis received the Democratic nomination, but George H. W. Bush soundly defeated him in November.

Gore returned to the Senate, $2 million in debt and facing his Senate reelection in two years. Not wanting to lose again, he reassessed his campaign and held critique sessions. In the meantime, he returned to one of his priorities—the environment.

Gore traveled to the South Pole, where scientists were taking tiny oxygen bubbles from ice core samples. They documented increasing levels of carbon dioxide within the ice, the result of pollution and man-made chlorofluorocarbons, or CFCs, used in aerosol-spray cans and refrigerants. Once released into the air, CFCs accumulate in the atmosphere, depleting the ozone layer that shields the Earth from the harmful effects of the sun's ultraviolet rays.

Gore also trekked to the Amazon to investigate the rain forest, where millions of trees produce oxygen for the planet, and thousands of types of birds and plants thrive. Gore and several scientists bathed in streams, slept in tents, and endured ticks and mosquitoes. They were concerned about the trees being cut down for farming and development.

When Gore returned to Washington he proposed the Strategic Environmental Initiative. His plan called for a complete phase out of CFCs within five years. He also advocated for massive reforestation programs, large-scale recycling programs, and studies to explore the development of alternative energy sources. Portions of Gore's plan were adopted a year later.

Global warming was Gore's main environmental concern. He held congressional hearings on the issue as scientific evidence suggested that as carbon dioxide created by cars and industry builds up in the earth's atmosphere it disrupts the earth's distribution of hot and cold. Scientists predict that as the earth's temperature rises the continental ice shelves will break up and severe weather, such as droughts, heat waves, and storms, will become more common. NASA scientist James Hansen predicted that by 2050 the Earth would warm by eight degrees Fahrenheit.

Gore also focused on several environmental disasters, such as the explosion of a nuclear reactor in Chernobyl, in the Ukraine, in 1986. The explosion sent a cloud of radioactive gas across northern and eastern Europe. Three years later the Exxon *Valdez,* an oil tanker, ran aground, spilling 11 million gallons of oil across the Alaskan coastline, killing hundreds of thousands of fish and birds.

As Gore worked on averting these global disasters, his family suffered a near tragedy. In April 1989, the Gores took

Although global warming was Gore's main environmental concern, he also focused on other environmental disasters, including the Exxon Valdez oil spill. *(Courtesy of the Exxon Valdez Oil Spill Trustee Council)*

their six-year-old son Albert to a baseball game. As they left the stadium, Albert pulled loose from his father's hand, ran into the street, and was struck by a car. He flew thirty feet into the air and sustained life-threatening injuries—broken ribs, a broken leg, and crushed internal organs.

Albert was in a coma for several days before regaining consciousness. During his three-month-long stay at Johns Hopkins Hospital in Baltimore he had surgeries to remove a portion of his spleen and to repair nerve damage in his arm. Gore moved into his son's hospital room, watching him around the clock.

When Albert returned home in a full-body cast, the Gores set up a hospital bed in their dining room. He still required intensive care from his parents and sisters day and night. Gradually, he mended, and the family healed too, helped by going to counseling. "It was a shattering experience for our whole family," Gore said. "And yet it has been in so many ways a great blessing for us. I never thought at the time I'd ever be able to say that. It completely changed my outlook on life."

Gore no longer took his family for granted. His son had nearly been killed and his daughters were growing older and would soon leave for college. His family had spent weeks apart

Gore carries his son, Albert. Albert was treated for life-threatening injuries he sustained after being hit by a car. *(Courtesy of AP Images/Carlos Osorio)*

Gore and Tipper wave as they participate in the 1988 St. Patrick's Day parade in Chicago. *(Courtesy of AP Images/Mark Elia)*

during his presidential run. Gore also realized that during his campaign, in order to win support, he had abandoned many of the issues important to him, such as the environment, children, and families. Although disappointed by his presidential loss, Albert's accident snapped his life into focus.

"When you've seen your six-year-old son fighting for his life, you realize that some things matter a lot more than winning," he said. "You lose patience with the lazy assumption of so many in politics that we can always just muddle through . . . you realize that we were not put here on earth to look out for our needs alone."

In the summer of 1990, Gore took a step towards spreading his environmental message. He signed a contract with the Houghton Mifflin publishing company to write *Earth in the Balance*. Fueled by Diet Coke, Gore wrote nights, weekends, and in his free hours. During one all-nighter Gore fell asleep, waking hours later to find that his elbow had hit the keyboard and typed the letter "r" thousands of times.

Earth in the Balance contained vivid descriptions of the environmental catastrophes facing the planet. He wrote about his visit to the Soviet Union's Aral Sea, formerly the most productive fishing site in central Asia. The Soviet government had attempted to divert the river to irrigate cotton fields. Now, where waves should have lapped, there was nothing but sand and giant steel ships dotting the dunes. He wrote of dolphins sickened from pollution and unable to resist viruses, and radioactive waters that killed millions of starfish. He also offered specific ideas to combat the destruction of rain forests, illegal dumping, greenhouse gases, and pesticides, and demanded that politicians propose tougher environmental regulations, even if they must endure political criticism.

"Every time I pause to consider whether I have gone too far out on a limb, I look at the new facts that continue to pour in from around the world and conclude that I have not gone nearly far enough," he wrote. "The integrity of the environment is not just another issue to be used in political games . . . And the time has long since come to take more political risks."

Although he considered retiring in 1990, Gore decided to remain in politics and try to affect changes in the areas he was most concerned about. He was reelected to the Senate. He also held firm to his priority of spending time with his family. A year later, as the 1992 presidential race heated up, he announced he wouldn't run for president. "I would like to be president,' he said, "but I am also a father, and I feel deeply about my responsibility to my children."

Few political candidates were eager to face President George H. W. Bush, who had overseen the Persian Gulf War that forced Iraqi dictator Saddam Hussein to pull his troops out of Kuwait, a neighboring oil-rich country. Hussein had invaded Iraq in August 1990, and President Bush, concerned about the oil supply, gave Hussein a deadline of January of 1991 to remove his forces from Kuwait. As the world waited to see if Saddam would remove the troops, Bush organized a large coalition of troops from around the world under the auspices of the United Nations. When the deadline passed, Bush ordered an invasion of Iraq. Air and ground attacks quickly defeated the Iraqi troops and liberated Kuwait. Following what seemed to be a quick and easy victory, Bush's popularity soared to 91 percent.

Former Massachusetts senator Paul Tsongas and former California governor Jerry Brown vied for the Democratic Party nomination. A third independent candidate, billionaire businessman H. Ross Perot, also entered the field. Political analysts suggested that if Gore changed his mind he would be the man to beat, but he refused to run.

In October of 1991, five-term Arkansas governor Bill Clinton declared himself a presidential candidate. A controversial figure, Clinton was accused of having extramarital affairs and of avoiding the draft in Vietnam. But he was a highly successful governor and had worked to improve education in Arkansas. He was also a gifted, even brilliant, politician who knew how to connect to the average voter.

Despite the so-called character issues that dogged his campaign, Bill Clinton quickly became the leading Democratic contender. He was obviously highly intelligent and had come from a humble background to become a Rhodes Scholar and a graduate of Yale Law School. He focused his campaign on issues close to voters' lives, such as the economy and improving education.

As the campaign carried on, it became obvious that President Bush's administration had significant problems that had been temporarily obscured by the victory in Iraq. When he had run for president in 1988 he had famously promised to not increase taxes. During his acceptance speech at the Republican Convention he had said: "Read my lips: No new taxes." This pledge helped get him elected, but when the economy faltered Bush approved a tax increase in 1990. This switch damaged his reputation, particularly with the more conservative members of his own party. Suddenly, President Bush looked vulnerable.

Although he was not running, Al Gore kept a keen eye on the campaigning. In June 1992, Bill Clinton locked up the Democratic nomination. He asked the influential lawyer Warren Christopher to be in charge of the search for a vice president. Christopher drafted a list of names and met with several Democrats, including Gore, to hear their opinions about who should be Clinton's running mate. Christopher asked Gore if he would be interested in the office. "It was a very guarded, reluctant response," Christopher remembered. "He said that was something he would have to think about for a long time."

Clinton whittled the list of vice presidential potentials down to a few names. With the Democratic National Convention a few weeks away he needed to make a decision. When Christopher asked Gore if he would meet with Clinton, Gore talked to his family. He might have more family time as vice president than as a senator. He would no longer have to return to Tennessee nearly every week, for one thing, and, with only a few months until the election in November, the campaign would be short. The opportunity to make a difference for his country also tempted him. They decided he should talk to Clinton.

It would be unconventional for Clinton to pick Gore. Most candidates picked someone from a different part of the country, or from a different wing of their party, to try to "balance" the ticket. They were from neighboring states, were close in age, and agreed on most issues.

The two men had met five years earlier, when Gore ran for president and sought Clinton's support but were not personally close. It was late in the day when Clinton met Gore in a Washington hotel. He had already interviewed the other potential candidates, but their conversation stretched beyond its scheduled end. Three hours later, Clinton asked Gore if he would consider being his running mate. Gore said he would happily accept, but emphasized he wanted a more active role than vice presidents typically had.

Throughout most of American history, the vice president had limited duties. He presided over the Senate and had the authority to break tie votes, but little other constitutional authority. Many vice presidents had suffered in the job. John Adams, the country's first vice president, called the position "the most insignificant office that ever the invention of man contrived or his imagination conceived . . . I can do neither good nor evil."

Gore wanted influence, especially on environmental, technological, and national security issues if he was going to leave the Senate to be vice president. He also wanted to meet with Clinton on a regular basis, and to ensure their two staffs were linked, so he would be kept apprised of all important meetings.

These were unprecedented requests, but Gore appealed to Clinton for many reasons. His intelligence and communication skills impressed Clinton, as well as Gore's familiarity with the ways of Washington. If he won, Clinton would come to the city as an outsider. He also liked Gore personally and respected that he was smart, funny, and loyal to both his family and his country. "Most importantly he won't stab you in the back," one of Gore's friends told Clinton, "even if you deserve it."

When an aide asked Clinton for another reason why he liked Gore, Clinton responded, "I could die, that's why." Clinton was confident in Gore's ability to assume the presidency if necessary.

When the news media learned Gore had made Clinton's short list of vice presidential candidates, reporters and photographers camped out on the edges of the property at Gore's farmhouse. They hoped to capture the event if Clinton chose Gore as his running mate.

On July 7, 1992, at 11:30 pm the phone rang inside the farmhouse. Both of the Gores were awake, and Tipper answered the phone. "Hi Tipper," Clinton said. "I hope I didn't wake you up; and if I did, I needed to."

Tipper handed the phone to her husband and Clinton asked Gore to be his running mate.

Excited and pleased, the Gores arranged to fly to Clinton's headquarters in Little Rock, Arkansas the following morning. Assuming they would be asleep, Gore chose not to call his parents, but, on the other side of the Caney Fork River, Al and Pauline Gore sat glued to the television until past 4:00

Gore and his family make their way to a plane bound for Little Rock, Arkansas, following Gore's acceptance of Bill Clinton's invitation to run as the Democratic vice presidential candidate. From left are: Gore, Tipper, Kristin, Albert, and Sarah. *(Courtesy of AP Images/Mark Humphrey)*

am, watching as their son's vice presidential path unfolded.

The next day, in the basement of the governor's mansion in Little Rock, Gore and Clinton discussed their vision for the country.

On July 15, 1992, at Madison Square Garden in New York Democratic officials nominated Clinton and Gore. Gore gave an impressive acceptance speech.

> All of us are part of something much greater than we are capable of imagining. And, my friends, if you look up for a moment from the rush of your daily lives, you will hear the quiet voices of your country crying out for help. You will see your reflection in the weary eyes of those who are losing hope

in America. And you will see that our democracy is lying there in the gutter waiting for us to give it a second breath of life.

After the Convention, the Clintons, Bill and his wife Hillary, and the Gores, boarded a campaign bus and began to travel through America. During fourteen-hour work days, they stopped and gave speeches, met people, and asked for votes. They also became stronger political partners and friends during the trip. The bus tour was a success and attracted a great deal of attention. People began to like the idea of voting for two young, ambitious, and intelligent men who were determined to bring about change.

When the two men and their wives began to appeal to younger crowds, the press nicknamed the campaign tour "Al and Bill's Excellent Adventure," after the popular movie, *Bill*

Gore (right) and Clinton make a campaign stop at a Texas café during Clinton's 1992 presidential campaign. *(Courtesy of AP Images/Stephan Savoia)*

and Ted's Excellent Adventure. Clinton and Gore reached out to young voters in other ways. Clinton played his saxophone on a late night television show and fielded questions on MTV. Tipper chased after reporters with water guns and played a joke on her husband during his interview on *Larry King Live.* Tipper called into the show, disguised her voice, and told Gore, "You're the most handsome man I've ever seen." King reminded the caller that the embarrassed Gore was happily married and not available for a date. "Not even with his wife?" Tipper responded, laughing.

During speeches, Gore often focused on the environment. He discussed a worldwide meeting, called the Earth Summit, held in Brazil in June of 1992, the first time world leaders met to address environmental concerns. The summit was a success, but while other countries willingly set targets to reduce carbon dioxide emissions, representatives of the Bush administration had dragged their feet. A frustrated Gore suggested that the United States had not only failed to lead but had actively fought against environmental progress.

"Our nation found itself embarrassed and isolated," Gore said. "The Bush administration insisted that our delegation argue in favor of so many nonsensical positions that a deadlock was virtually guaranteed."

The Republican candidates ridiculed Gore for his environmental stance, labeling him an extremist and calling him "Ozone Man." Gore retaliated, citing the destruction of the ozone shield, the poisoning of air and water from pollution, and the loss of more than one acre every second in the rain forest because of foresting.

As the election drew closer, Clinton and Gore's polling numbers improved. The addition of Gore had clearly helped

Bill Clinton (left) and George H. W. Bush speak during a 1992 presidential debate. *(Courtesy of AP Images/Doug Mills)*

the Clinton's campaign. Gore helped in areas in which Clinton was weak. He had experience in Washington and a strong marriage. He also voluntarily served in the Vietnam War and had supported the Persian Gulf War.

Gore's intelligence also highlighted the shortcomings of the current vice president, Dan Quayle. Quayle had become a favorite of late night comedians for his public blunders. In one classroom visit that became infamous, Quayle informed a young boy that he had misspelled the word *potato* and told him to add *e* to the end, *potatoe.*

"Gore has written a book," quipped one Democratic senator, "and Quayle can't spell."

Before the 1992 election, several Republicans urged George Bush to take Quayle off the ticket. They were dismayed when he refused. "Both of the Democratic candidates are young and smart, and we've only got one of each," groused one Republican campaign official.

Tipper also was an asset to the campaign. Hillary Clinton was almost as controversial, and reviled by some conservatives for continuing her work as a lawyer during her husband's political career. Tipper was heralded as the "anti-Hillary" because she had left her public career to raise her children. Even her work as a "crusading housekeeper," establishing the PMRC was praised.

The Clinton/Gore campaign encountered its share of rough spots, however. In one vice presidential debate Quayle attacked Clinton's personal character. Clinton's advisers criticized Gore for not saying more to defend Clinton. They also disapproved of Gore's formal and often stilted speaking style, which contrasted with Clinton's humorous, relaxed speeches. Gore also had leaped into his more active role as a vice presidential candidate, and sometimes irritated Clinton's high-strung chief tactician James Carville.

"That Gore! He has an opinion on everything we're doing! And he thinks we oughta do *this* different. And he thinks we oughta do *that* different! He's driving me crazy!" Carville ranted. "But I'll tell you something. I'll still take him over anybody else! Because he is the most disciplined, on-message person I have ever worked with."

When Election Day 1992 finally rolled around, Gore flew back to Nashville. He landed at 2:00 am and fell into bed. After he woke and ate breakfast, he jogged to his parent's farm. That afternoon he voted, stopping to chat with Alota Thompson, who had watched him many summers ago.

President-elect Bill Clinton and Vice President-elect Gore celebrate with their families after winning the presidential election. *(Courtesy of AP Images/Susan Ragan)*

By that night it was clear that voters across the country had elected Bill Clinton president and Al Gore vice president. Clinton was the youngest man elected president, and the first Democrat elected since Jimmy Carter in 1976.

For the past sixteen years the Gores had lived in Arlington, Virginia. Now they moved to the vice president's residence, the one-hundred-year-old Admiralty House, on the grounds of the U.S. Naval Observatory in Washington, D.C.

six
Inside the White House

On January 20, 1993, with one hand on his sister Nancy's Bible, Albert Gore Jr. was sworn in as the vice president of the United States. He had stayed up most of the night before helping to write Clinton's inaugural address.

Gore and Clinton wanted to begin work immediately. Despite their busy schedules, he and Clinton met weekly for lunch. Gore's office was close to the Oval Office, and his staff merged with Clinton's to better coordinate communication.

Clinton and Gore decided his first task should be to try to streamline the federal government. Presidential candidate, billionaire H. Ross Perot, had run for president on the platform that the government was wasting taxpayers' money and needed to be downsized—and had captured 9 percent of the votes. Clearly, it was an issue people cared about.

Gore created a committee and they began to meet and talk with government workers. The waste and mismanagement

Gore gives a speech during a ceremony for the Reinventing Government initiative, a plan proposed by Gore to cut down on government spending and waste. (*Courtesy of Andrea Booher/FEMA*)

within the government amazed him. "A federal worker told me that twenty-three separate people had to sign off on one requisition for a PC [personal computer]," Gore said. "So, it's a whole dysfunctional system."

By September 1993, Gore had hammered out a plan. He proposed eliminating thousands of unnecessary jobs, offering money-saving incentives to individual government agencies, and giving them more independent authority to hire and promote workers.

Four years later, Gore would publish a book detailing some of his work on restructuring the government. *Businesslike Government: Lessons Learned from America's Best Companies,* which detailed dozens of meetings Gore held with top executives and management experts. He discussed key principles that needed to be applied to the federal government.

Another one of Gore's achievements involved the North American Free Trade Agreement, or NAFTA. NAFTA was intended to limit trade barriers between North American countries. The Clinton administration supported its approval and insisted it would increase job opportunities and investment. H. Ross Perot, who still held the nation's ear, argued that if NAFTA were passed Americans would lose jobs to lower-paid Mexican workers. The Clinton administration worried that Perot could sway Congress to not pass NAFTA.

Perot accepted Gore's invitation to debate NAFTA on *Larry King Live.* Gore prepared for the debate by studying. Perot's warning about the destructive impact NAFTA would

President Bill Clinton signs legislation implementing NAFTA as (from left) Gore, House Minority Leader Bob Michel, and House Speaker Thomas Foley applaud. *(Courtesy of AP Images/Doug Mills)*

have, and even held mock debates. The preparation paid off. He refuted Perot's claims point-by-point during the debate.

"The Vice President of the United States had to be trained all weekend to be arrogant, condescending, and rude," Perot flustered. Perot, who had spent most of his life running his business, was used to people listening to what he said and agreeing. He was not used to having his ideas challenged and soon lost his temper, making a bad impression. In many ways, his encounter with Gore effectively ended his influence as a public official, though he ran for president agan in 1996.

In November of 1993, Republicans and Democrats voted to pass NAFTA. Gore had played a large role in the administration's success.

Gore quickly became one of Clinton's closest advisors. Gore knew the political, social, and technical workings of Washington, and he helped guide Clinton, who had no experience with the U.S. Congress. He also revised Clinton's speeches, critiqued his performances, and recommended staffing changes. Clinton didn't always take Gore's advice, but Gore wasn't afraid to speak his mind.

Although the two men worked well together, they were different in several ways. Gore was a disciplined, reserved, determined worker. Clinton was an equally hard worker but had trouble keeping on a schedule and often kept late hours. He was also more outgoing and more of a natural politician than Gore.

During his first four years as vice president, Gore made his mark. He negotiated a deal with the Ukraine, getting them to surrender their nuclear warheads. He also helped pass the Telecommunications Act in 1996. The bill required V-chips in all new televisions, which allowed parents to screen out

Although Gore and Clinton were different in many ways, they worked closely together during most of Clinton's presidency. *(Courtesy of AP Images/Greg Gibson)*

programs they thought were unsuitable for their children. It also set fines and jail terms for people who made indecent material available online to children. Clinton signed Gore's bill with the same pen Dwight D. Eisenhower used to sign the bill that created the interstate highway system, which had been sponsored in the Senate by Al Gore Sr.

Gore also introduced a measure to improve the nation's computer networking infrastructure, helping to pave the way for the Internet. He set up a Web site called *Welcome to the Whitehouse: An Interactive Citizen's Handbook* where visitors could access government information, take visual tours of the White House, and find out about government Web sites and services.

The Gores made efforts to have regular family dinners and attend their children's school events. They played badminton on the manicured lawn of their new house and enjoyed family movie nights at the IMAX theater in the National Air and Space Museum.

In 1994, Tipper began her own project. She teamed up with physician's assistant Pat Letke-Alexander to help take homeless mentally ill people to facilities where they could receive care. The two women met in the morning and began their route through local parks, looking for people who suffered from schizophrenia, depression, and bipolar disorders. Tipper coaxed a man known as Captain Kersh, who fought in Vietnam, into a shelter. When she visited, she brought him a letter from her husband, saying he was proud of the man's progress and signed as a fellow veteran. At the hospital, she and Letke-Alexander talked to the resident doctor, while a nearby patient ranted in the background. There was "the crazy lazy behind us, the resident in front of us, nobody having a clue who Tipper is, and she's just acting like it's totally normal," said Letke-Alexander, describing the scene.

At times Tipper invited her mentally ill friends for lunch at the Naval Observatory. After the meal Captain Kersh and others often went outside to smoke the cigarette butts they had found on the streets. "Nice house," one named Jack commented to Letke-Alexander. "Her husband must have a nice job."

"Well he does," she answered. "He's the vice president."

"Oh," said Jack, as if it was no big deal, which was exactly how Tipper wanted it.

Tipper also continued her photography. In August 1996, she published *Picture This: A Visual Diary,* which contained pictures taken during the first four years of the Clinton administration, featuring everything from personal images to pictures of places Tipper had traveled internationally.

During the first term, the Gores also helped the Clintons endure many personal upheavals. The First Lady's father suffered a stroke and passed away. Vincent Foster, the deputy White House counsel and a close friend of the Clintons, committed suicide. The Clintons also struggled with accusations that they were involved in shady real estate dealings while Clinton was governor. During this time, Bill Clinton's mother, Virginia Kelley passed away.

Shortly after her death, Republican Senate Majority Leader Bob Dole appeared on television. He praised Clinton's mother, then launched into an attack, demanding that a special prosecutor be appointed to look into the Clinton's real estate dealings.

Gore responded to Dole publicly: "Now doesn't it bother you a little bit to have the president attending the funeral service of his mother," he said, "and to have members of the political opposition, as the service is going on . . . making these attacks?"

Although independent prosecutor Kenneth Starr found no evidence to charge the Clintons with wrongdoings during the real estate dealings, Clinton continued to endure unprecedented scrutiny into his private life. A former Arkansas state employee had filed a law suit against him, claiming Clinton sexually harassed her while he served as governor.

The administration suffered other, less personal, setbacks. After a bitter struggle they were able to pass an economic plan that began the process of balancing the federal budget, but the administration failed its goal of ensuring health care for every American. Hillary Clinton had headed up the health care initiative by gathering a large group of expert advisors, including Tipper as an advisor on mental health. But a massive, heavily financed campaign against it by large insurance and pharmaceutical companies, killed the health care plan in Congress.

The failure of health care, and the fierce attacks by Republicans in Congress, tore away at the administration's popularity. On Election Day 1994, Democrats suffered their worst defeat ever and lost control of the House and the Senate, as well as being defeated in gubernatorial races around the country.

Undeterred, Clinton was determined to be reelected president in 1996, and he needed Gore's help. They met regularly to discuss strategies, personnel, and advertising. Gore began to make calls to Democratic contributors asking for financial backing.

If Clinton won reelection, Gore would be poised to run for president in 2000. Despite the pressure the two men were

Bob Dole challenged President Clinton in the 1996 presidential election. *(Courtesy of AP Images/Stephan Savoia)*

under, they still had a sense of humor, especially about Gore's future. For Gore's birthday in March of 1996, Clinton gave him fake keys to Air Force One and a photo from the State of the Union address with their faces switched to show Gore as the president and Clinton as the vice president.

In 1996, Clinton and Gore faced Republican nominee Bob Dole, from Kansas. Dole was a gruff World War II veteran in his seventies who had served in Congress for more than thirty years. Dole had challenged Ronald Reagan for the presidential nomination in 1980 and George Bush in 1988 and had lost both times. An early favorite, Dole chose former Representative Jack Kemp as his running mate.

In the summer of 1996, Democrats gathered in Chicago, Illinois for the national convention. Gore gave vibrant speeches when he and Clinton appeared together after the convention. After one of Gore's humorous, rapid-fire speeches Clinton began his follow-up speech by wondering what Gore ate for breakfast that had given him so much energy.

They kept up the energy and in November, Clinton and Gore won 59 percent of the vote. In his victory speech, Clinton called Gore the finest vice president America ever had.

The second Clinton administration was filled with controversy as well as success. Soon after the election critics questioned the work Gore did raising money for the campaign. Soliciting contributions in federal buildings is illegal. In March of 1997, Gore appeared on television and admitted his mistake, but he appeared stiff and unapologetic. Attorney General Janet Reno investigated the fundraising.

Three months later, environmental groups attacked Gore for not enacting tougher air pollution standards. They warned Gore it would be good for his political future if he listened to them, otherwise they wouldn't support him for president. "Don't go down that road," Gore responded firmly. "I am committed to this cause, and I am not going to decide what we should do based on whether it will get me elected."

All was not partisan warfare. In July of 1997, Gore's oldest daughter, Karenna, married Andrew Schiff, a doctor from New York. Friends and family gathered at the National Cathedral for the wedding.

In December 1997, world leaders met in Kyoto, Japan to discuss environmental issues. The European Union wanted all industrial nations to cut their emissions to 15 percent below 1990 levels by the year 2010. The Clinton administration planned to cut emissions to 1990 levels by 2012. Several developing countries, such as China, India, and Brazil, wanted exemption from the emission standards because it would impede their economic growth.

The 1997 environmental treaty conference in Kyoto, Japan *(Courtesy of AP Images/Katsumi Kasahara)*

Gore was pressured from all sides not to attend the treaty. Business groups argued the treaty threatened the economic gains made in the Clinton years, environmental groups clamored the Kyoto treaty was not strict enough, and the nations in Europe insisted on the 2010 deadline and wanted the United States to agree to stricter emission cuts. The leaders in the Senate said it would not ratify the treaty if developing countries didn't shoulder some of the responsibility for limiting greenhouse gases. Bob Squier, Gore's trusted consultant, told him that getting involved in the Kyoto treaty was political suicide.

But without support from the White House, Gore feared the talks would collapse; the environmental issues he believed in and fought for would suffer an enormous setback. He decided to take the political risk and went to Kyoto. Gore promised the U.S. would decrease its emissions 7 percent below 1990 levels by the year 2012. The countries also agreed on an international trading system in which pollution permits could be bought and sold, giving companies incentives to cut emissions.

When the treaty was presented to the Senate for ratification it essentially died on arrival. Republicans controlled both houses of Congress and were not inclined to pass many of the Clinton administration's initiatives, and business groups came out strongly against the Kyoto treaty, claiming it would lead to the loss of an astronomical number of jobs, although, there was little evidence to back up their claims.

One study estimated that compliance with the treaty would lead to a rise in the cost of gasoline and higher energy bills for the average American household. The White House took the stance that the ultimate costs of noncompliance were higher, but the leaders in Congress said they would block any funding initiatives that introduced new regulations that were in compliance with the treaty. Several countries ratified the Kyoto treaty and adhere to its standards, but the U.S. still refuses to do so.

Environmentalists were disappointed when the Senate rejected the treaty, but most of them realized Gore had done the best he could. "It was the most courageous and important thing that Al Gore has ever done," said Greg Wetstone of the Natural Resources Defense Council. "He took the risk of personally going, inserting himself, and ultimately securing an intelligent agreement."

The fundraising controversy continued to dog Gore, but in December 1997 he was vindicated when the attorney general ruled that the fundraising calls had not violated the law. Gore attempted to put the campaign fundraising scandal behind him and to move on. But there was no escaping the scandals and accusations that swirled around Washington. Soon the administration was rocked by investigations into President Clinton's sex life.

The investigations were first authorized to look into a land deal the Clintons were involved in years before he was elected president, but after the Republicans took over Congress it spread in several directions and continued for four years. When the president was forced to give a deposition in the Paula Jones's lawsuit he was asked questions about his relationship with another woman, a young former White House intern named Monica Lewinksy. Clinton denied any relationship with Lewinsky. Later, it was revealed that they had had an intimate relationship.

At first, Gore believed the president's denial of the relationship and defended Clinton publicly. However, he did attempt to distance himself from the scandal in more subtle ways that did not go unnoticed by the president and Hillary Clinton.

In April 1998, a federal judge dismissed Jones's lawsuit against Clinton, but three months later reports surfaced that Monica Lewinsky planned to admit to an affair with the president and presented evidence to prove it.

There is no law forbidding extramarital sex, but the special prosecutor Kenneth Starr, who had the support of the Republican Congress, issued a report that detailed every aspect of the affair in intimate detail. He also said that the president had committed "high crimes and misdemeanors" sufficient to justify removal of office by lying under oath about the affair.

Clearly, one of the intentions of the Starr Report was to embarrass Clinton and to outrage the public and create support for Clinton's impeachment and conviction. Clinton countered by admitting to the affair in a television confession. But he also said it was a personal family matter and that even presidents deserve private lives. Essentially, he admitted to lying but implied Starr and his lawyers were asking him about things that were none of their business.

After Starr's report was released, and Clinton addressed the nation, there was one question before the American people: did lying about a personal indiscretion justify removing a president from office?

At the time of Clinton's confession, Gore was in Hawaii on vacation. Thirty-six hours later he issued a supportive, but carefully worded, statement. He praised the president for his courage in admitting the scandal, reaffirmed their friendship, and praised Clinton's record in office.

Although all the public opinion polls showed that while the majority of the American people were upset and disappointed with the president, they overwhelmingly did not want him to be impeached. But the intensity of the partisan war between the Democratic president and the Republican Congress had grown too large to be contained by public opinion. The House of Representatives passed the articles of impeachment and the case went to the Senate to be tried.

If Clinton was convicted in the Senate he would be removed from office and Gore would become president, but Gore spoke out against removing Clinton at every opportunity. He also urged everyone to rally around the president. However, he was disappointed in his friend and colleague. When Clinton apologized personally to his staff, Gore was blunt. "Mr. President, I think most of America has forgiven you, but you've got to get your act together," Gore warned.

On December 5, 1998, in the middle of the political upheaval, ninety-year-old Al Gore Sr. passed away. Family, friends, and political figures attended the funeral.

The vote in the Senate was never in doubt. On February 12, 1999, Clinton was found not guilty on both of the articles of impeachment. It was clear that his adversaries had overstepped. The Republicans lost seats in Congress in the 1998 midterm elections, and throughout the ordeal, Clinton's job approval rating actually increased to 60 percent.

Clinton had avoided removal from office, but his reputation was tarnished. The president's problems tainted Gore, putting the vice-president's political future at risk. Until late in the summer of 1998, Gore's presidential run, and probable victory, had seemed assured. The country was at peace, the economy was enjoying unprecedented growth, and the federal budget was balanced for the first time in decades.

Now Gore's future was not so certain. Although he had been cleared of the fund-raising allegations, his image as a squeaky clean politician had been damaged. After the Lewinsky scandal, he became quietly angry about Clinton's recklessness, which threatened both the president's marriage and his administration. Although Clinton admitted his mistakes, the relationship between them had been permanently damaged. While they continued to hold their weekly lunches, Gore was less of a presence. He no longer ran down the hall to join unexpected meetings. One good piece of news was that polls showed people didn't hold Gore accountable for Clinton's behavior; 63 percent of American people thought Gore was trustworthy, while 23 percent felt the same about Clinton.

As the Clinton administration wound down, Gore made a decision and announced he would run for president in 2000. Only two sitting vice presidents had ever been elected president—Martin Van Buren in 1836, and George Bush in 1988. Even so, he confidently took the first step toward the presidency. It was a path he had trod once before, but this time he planned to end it successfully.

seven

A Valiant Battle

O n June 15, 1999, Al Gore Jr. began his presidential campaign in the way that he and his father
began many campaigns, standing on the steps of
the courthouse in Carthage, Tennessee. As crowd of 5,000
people cheered, he spoke in front of billowing American
flags and the old red brick courthouse.

The favorite on the Republican side was two-term Texas
governor George W. Bush, son of the former president.
Challenging Gore for the Democratic nomination was New
Jersey senator and former basketball star Bill Bradley.

Polling numbers suggested that Clinton's problems con-
tinued to haunt Gore. Voters were tired of the drama in the
White House, and 40 percent of the people who approved of
Gore planned to vote for Bush.

Gore attempted to distance himself from Clinton. While
he praised Clinton's economic and foreign policy achievements, he, for the first time in public, called the president's

personal actions inexcusable. He even admitted that he had suspected Clinton wasn't revealing the entire story about Monica Lewinsky from the beginning. At other times, unsure of his best move politically, he lightened the condemnations and welcomed Clinton's campaign efforts.

In the first half of the campaign, Gore made mistakes. He had trouble getting his staff together. He also focused too much on Bush, instead of Bradley, who was his immediate opponent. The campaign was adrift and off to a wobbly start as he tried to address meaty issues, such as improving education, funding cancer research, and fighting drug abuse.

Bradley's connections on Wall Street and in professional sports helped him raise $11.5 million. Gore had raised $18.5 million but was spending it as fast as it came in. By September they were tied in the polls in New Hampshire, formerly considered an easy state for Gore. Bradley's volunteers had distributed 100,000 leaflets, knocked on 35,000 doors, and spoken to 10,000 people. He offered hope for Democrats who were upset with Clinton and unsure of Gore.

Now considered the underdog, Gore used a new approach. He dropped the rigid blue suits that caused some to view as him as boring, and replaced some staff members. He moved his headquarters to Nashville, away from competing political agendas in Washington. The move gave the campaign a breath of fresh air. Invoking Gandhi to explain his motives, Gore said, "You must become the change you wish to see in the world. I want this campaign to become the change we're fighting for."

He became again the Al Gore who had once campaigned at diners and pancake houses. Before long, he regained his lead over Bradley, winning the Democratic nomination.

He chose Connecticut senator Joseph Lieberman, the first national Jewish candidate in the country's history, as his running mate.

In the November election, Gore and Lieberman faced George W. Bush and his vice presidential running mate Dick Cheney, who had been secretary of defense under Bush's father. Bush aimed to join the only other father and son in history to both become president—John Adams in 1796 and his son John Quincy Adams in 1825. Also running were the liberal Green Party candidate Ralph Nader, and the conservative Reform Party candidate Pat Buchanan. As the election approached, polls showed Bush having a slight lead over

Gore and Tipper wave to supporters at a rally held during Gore's 2000 election campaign. *(Courtesy of AP Images/J. Scott Applewhite)*

Gore. By Election Day the numbers were too close to call.

Both Gore and Bush campaigned vigorously in Michigan, Pennsylvania, and Florida, large swing states with a high number of Electoral College votes. In the Electoral College system, voters are actually choosing an elector pledged to support one candidate. Each state's number of electoral votes is determined by adding its number of congressmen and two senators. States with higher populations have more electoral votes. Florida was important because it had twenty-five electoral votes. Many believed Bush held the advantage in Florida because his brother Jeb was the state's governor, but Florida also had a number of strongly Democratic counties.

On Election Day 2000 nearly 100 million Americans went to the polls. Some waited in long lines to elect the forty-third president. As the day wore on, exit poll results began to trickle in. Exit pollsters ask people about their votes as they left the polling site, and news networks use their results to predict a winner before all votes are counted. For exit polls to be accurate a large enough sample of people need to be polled. Usually the results reflect how the nation votes, but in a close election there is a higher risk of error.

By 7:49 pm eastern standard time, news services were projecting that Gore had won Florida, a likely fatal blow for Bush's chances of winning. The Bush family expected to win in Florida and was gathered in a Texas hotel suite watching the election returns and dining on fried chicken, shrimp, and ice cream. The Florida projection ended the festivities and the family retired to the Texas governor's mansion, where Bush could be in closer contact with his campaign headquarters. The news distressed them because the networks made their projections before results came in from

Florida's panhandle, which was heavily Republican. Bush worried that if Florida's Republican voters thought Gore won the state they might choose not to vote, convinced that their votes wouldn't matter.

By 9:00 pm the networks declared Gore the winner in both Michigan and Pennsylvania, the two other closely contested swing states. Despite the good news, Gore continued campaigning from his hotel room in Nashville. He called key radio stations in western states, where the polls were still open, and urged people to vote for him.

During the night the race grew tighter as votes for Bush had begun to add up in Florida. By 10:00 pm news services said Florida was too close to call and retracted their projection. "The networks giveth and the networks taketh away," commented one anchorperson.

It soon became clear that neither candidate would win the election without taking Florida. Across the nation people stayed up into the morning waiting to find out which candidate had won. By 1:00 am Bush led in Florida by 250,000 votes, but some largely Democratic counties remained uncounted. At 2:16 am networks made the critical call that Bush had won Florida. Gore called Bush to concede the election.

Within another hour it appeared the networks had made another error. Bush's lead in Florida had slipped to just hundreds of votes. According to Florida law, if the margin fell below half of 1 percent of the vote there had to be a recount. The networks realized their mistake and took back their projection for a second time. Gore's advisors informed him of the new development, catching him just before he made his concession speech. At 3:15 a.m. he called Bush to withdraw his concession. Gore's staff encircled him and listened to the conversation.

"Circumstances have changed dramatically since I first called you," Gore said. "The state of Florida is too close to call."

"Are you saying what I think you're saying?" Bush responded. "Let me make sure that I understand. You're calling me back to retract that concession?"

"You don't have to be snippy about it," Gore retorted. Bush said his brother Jeb had assured him he won the state.

"Let me explain something," Gore said stiffly, "Your little brother is not the ultimate authority on this."

"You do what you have to do," Bush said, ending the conversation.

When Gore turned to his silent staff and smiled, the room exploded in cheers.

The Florida election had been plagued with problems all day. There were a large number

The results of the 2000 presidential election were so inconclusive the news media had trouble determining a clear winner. The *Orlando Sentinel* published four different editions on the day after the elections.
(Courtesy of AP Images/Peter Cosgrove)

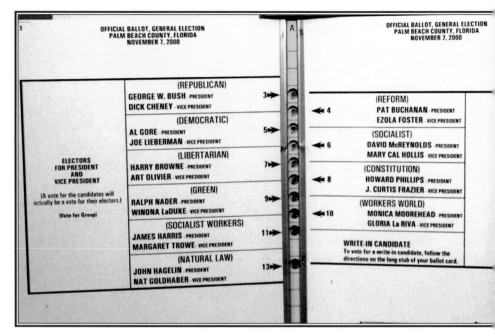

Many criticized the Palm Beach County butterfly ballot as difficult to understand.

of malfunctioning voting machines and late-opening polling sites, primarily in poorer neighborhoods.

In Palm Beach County many criticized the way the ballot was formatted because it was difficult to understand. Called a butterfly ballot, it looked like an open book, with the candidates' names on opposite sides of the ballot and punch holes down the center. But the punch holes for each candidate were close together, which made it easy to vote for the wrong candidate, particularly for the large number of elderly voters in the county. Often voters who realized their mistake tried to remedy it by punching the ballot again. nineteen thousand double-punched ballots were declared invalid and not counted; another 10,000 ballots came in with the presidential line accidentally left blank.

When Burt Aaronson, the Democratic County Commissioner in Palm Beach, voted, he called over to his wife on the other side of the curtain, "It's a tricky ballot. Be careful."

Workers at polling sites in Palm Beach fielded complaints and tried to reach Theresa LePore, the supervisor of elections, who had approved the butterfly ballot. Angry voters descended on her office. Natalie Zeller, Gore's campaign manager in Tallahassee, Florida, tried calling LePore several times. All sixty-five phone lines into her office were busy. When she finally reached her, LePore said in a quiet voice that she knew of the problems.

As more problems in Florida came to light, the country wondered how much incompetence on the part of elected officials altered the election's results. There were also accusations that highway patrol officers and poll workers had discouraged African American voters from voting by setting up vehicle checkpoints near polling sites and telling them they weren't registered to vote when they were.

Florida's mechanical voting machines also raised questions. Mechanical vote counts were never entirely accurate, and in such a close race even a small degree of inaccuracy could change the election results. Gore argued that only a hand count would show voters' true intent because a machine would miss partially punched ballots. At the Democrats' request, the largely Democratic counties began counting votes by hand. Bush retaliated, saying he had won the first ballot count and that a hand count was subject to tampering and errors.

Both candidates sent legal teams to Florida to represent their interests. Warren Christopher, Clinton's secretary of state,

This Broward County canvassing board member examines an election ballot. *(Courtesy of AP Images/Alan Diaz)*

argued that a recount would show Gore as the true winner. Bush's representative, former Secretary of State James Baker, disagreed, and argued that Bush had won in the polling booths. Both sides took their arguments to court.

As lawyers, journalists, and politicians protested the voting irregularities, Gore supporters took to the streets, carrying signs protesting the confusing ballots with slogans such as "Gore Got More," "Revote," and "This is Not a Game"

The debate continued in the courts. Bush's lawyers argued that there were no statewide standards to guide a hand recount and that a ballot counted in one county might be discounted in another. Particularly in question were ballots in which the chad, the part of the ballot punched out, was incompletely or partly punched out. These were soon called *hanging chads.*

On November 13, a federal court upheld Bush's attempt to block the hand counts. Florida secretary of state Katherine Harris said she would enforce the deadline of November 14 for vote tallies, as set by the Florida legislature. Only absentee ballots, which were due by November 17, would be added to the totals after that date.

Harris's involvement soon became controversial. She was the co-chair of Bush's campaign in Florida, and Democrats were convinced she was determined to stop the recounts, instead of operating in a nonpartisan neutral manner as laid out in the state constitution. When one court decision supported Katherine Harris's involvement, Gore's team of lawyers took the case to Florida's Supreme Court, and on November 17 it ruled that Katherine Harris was prohibited from immediately certifying the results of the election. A judge ruled that hand counts needed to be included in the final vote tallies, setting a deadline of November 26 for all of the hand counts to be finished.

Bush's team appealed the decision to the U.S. Supreme Court, which overturned the Florida court's decision. By November 26, Katherine Harris certified the vote tallies and declared Bush the winner of Florida and the election. Officially, Bush had won Florida by less than half of one thousandth of 1 percent.

Bush publicly asked Gore to concede. "Now that the votes are counted," Bush said. "It's time for the votes to count."

Gore's team insisted that the vote tallies were inaccurate. Miami-Dade County hadn't finished their hand recount and claimed they had been intimidated into stopping by rowdy demonstrators bused in by Republicans. Palm Beach County officials didn't finish their recount either, and took the Thanksgiving holiday off, despite the rapidly approaching deadline. Katherine Harris refused to accept the numbers from the partial hand recounts and wouldn't extend the deadline. The recount was stopped with 1,000 questionable ballots unchecked. Then, over Thanksgiving, officials in Florida's Nassau County suddenly discovered a suspiciously large number of previously uncounted ballots for Bush. Democrats objected to this, calling it the Thanksgiving Surprise.

Gore's team headed back to court to overturn the certified election results.

Florida's Supreme Court ordered a hand recount in all Florida counties that failed to tabulate "under votes"—ballots that machine counts hadn't registered as votes for either candidate. This was Gore's last victory. Bush's attorneys took the case to the U.S. Supreme Court. The justices stopped the recounts on the grounds it violated the Equal Protection Clause of the Fourteenth Amendment of the U.S. Constitution, which guaranteed that state laws be applied to everyone in the same way.

These protesters stand outside the U.S. Supreme Court during the proceedings of the *Bush v. Gore* case. *(Courtesy of AP Images/Steve Helber)*

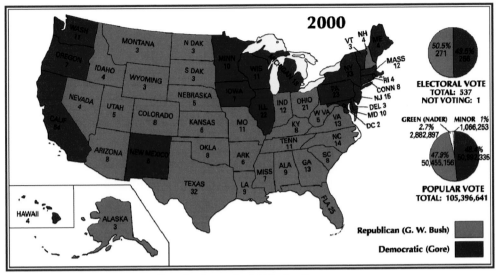

2000

WASH 11
MONTANA 3
N DAK 3
MINN 10
WIS 11
MICHIGAN 18
VT 3
NH 4
ME 4
OREGON 7
IDAHO 4
WYOMING 3
S DAK 3
IOWA 7
NY 33
MASS 12
NEVADA 4
UTAH 5
COLORADO 8
NEBRASKA 5
ILL 22
IND 12
OHIO 21
PA 23
RI 4
CONN 8
NJ 15
CALIF 54
ARIZONA 8
NEW MEXICO 8
KANSAS 6
MO 11
KY 8
W VA 5
VA 13
DEL 3
MD 10
DC 2
OKLA 8
ARK 6
TENN 11
NC 14
SC 8
TEXAS 32
MISS 7
ALA 9
GA 13
LA 9
FLA 25
HAWAII 4
ALASKA 3

50.5% 271 49.5% 266
ELECTORAL VOTE
TOTAL: 537
NOT VOTING: 1

GREEN (NADER) MINOR 1%
2.7% 1,066,253
2,882,897

47.9% 48.4%
50,455,156 50,992,335

POPULAR VOTE
TOTAL: 105,396,641

Republican (G. W. Bush)
Democratic (Gore)

Results from the 2000 election

The Supreme Court decision in the case, called *Bush v. Gore*, was a 5-4 vote that broke down on party lines. The five justices appointed by Republican presidents voted on Bush's side, the four Democratic appointees supported Gore. Many Democrats believed that members of the Supreme Court had given in to their personal partisan loyalties. But Gore had said before that he would abide by the Supreme Court's final ruling.

"Now the Supreme Court has spoken . . . While I strongly disagree with the Court's position, I accept it," Gore said in his concession speech on December 13. "Just moments ago, I spoke to George Bush and congratulated him on becoming the forty-third president of the United States—and I promised him that I wouldn't call him back this time," he added.

Gore had often turned to his father for political advice. Now, in his moment of loss, he again turned to the words of the man who had offered him both strength and encouragement throughout his political career.

"As for the battle that ends tonight," he said when he conceded. "I do believe, as my father once said, that no matter how hard the loss, defeat might serve as well as victory to shape the soul and let the glory out."

After his speech Gore, descended the granite steps of the Old Executive Office Building, across the alley from the White House. Cameras flashed as he passed several hundred of his staffers who waited in the cold and cheered him.

The election had been a difficult ordeal for the nation. It had taken five weeks to decide, while Americans wondered who would be the next president. It was the most turbulent and closest election in modern U.S. history. Gore won the popular vote with 50,996,582 votes to Bush's 50,456,062. Because of the Electoral College system, however, a presidential candidate can win more of the popular votes and still lose the election.

Gore was the first presidential candidate since Grover Cleveland in 1888 to win the popular vote and lose the election. Bush was in league with only three other presidents who had lost the popular vote—John Quincy Adams, Rutherford B. Hayes, and Benjamin Harrison—but won the election.

The results encouraged people to examine how future elections were conducted. On May 4, 2001, the Florida legislature approved an election reform bill, banning punch-card voting systems and enacting uniform polling-place procedures to ensure voters were treated fairly. Other states examined their procedures too.

National task forces were set up to study voting methods and election standards. The U.S. Commission on Civil Rights investigated possibilities that voting rights had been violated for minorities. The unsettling results showed that African

Americans in Florida were nine times more likely to have their ballots rejected in the counting process.

The Election Center, a nonprofit group that assists election officials, suggested several changes, such as uniform rules for recounts. They also recommended that the media not project election results prior to 11 p.m. eastern standard time. The center suggested poll workers be trained so they are sensitive to different races and disabilities.

Regardless of the changes and reforms, the 2000 election was long over, and on January 1, 2001, George W. Bush was sworn in as the forty-third president.

eight
A Call for Change

On December 14, 2000, the day after Al Gore's concession speech, he slept until 11 a.m., exhausted after the grueling campaign and recount. Over the next months he virtually dropped out of sight, traveling with Tipper for six weeks in Spain, Greece, and Italy. He wore dark glasses and a baseball cap tugged down low, and he grew what many called a mountain man beard. He wanted to be with his family and out of the scrutinizing public eye.

Gore and his family returned to Tennessee after their vacation, and he and Tipper bought a hundred-year-old house in Nashville. The settled in quickly, with Tipper's drums resting in the living room next to a wall of photographs showing Gore as vice president. They still owned Tipper's grandfather's house in Virginia and their ninety-acre farm in Carthage.

Gore eventually emerged and began to appear more in public, calling himself a recovering politician. He started teaching, dividing his duties between Columbia University's

Gore lectures students about environmental issues at Middle
Tennessee State University in this 2004 photo. *(Courtesy of AP Images/John
Russell)*

Graduate School of Journalism in New York, Middle
Tennessee State University, Fisk University in Nashville,
and University of California, Los Angeles. He met with
students and faculty and worked to develop a curriculum
focusing on families and community building. He planned
to bring together experts in education, business, and public
policy to work on society's problems.

Gore often spoke in public, appearing mainly in classrooms.
He usually warmed up with a few jokes. "Hi, I'm Al Gore. I
used to be the next President of the United States." When people
laughed, he dryly added, "I don't find that particularly funny."

Another favorite was, "You know the old saying. You win
some, you lose some—and then there's that little known third
category."

Gore was in the third category, but making the most of it.
Sometimes people approached him who despaired of Bush's

win. They called Gore, "Mr. President." Others told him, "We know you really won."

Gore entered the business world. He became an advisor for the Internet search company Google, and a board member for Apple Inc. With partner Joel Hyatt he started Current TV, a news network geared toward people in their twenties. Also with another partner, David Blood, Gore helped to start Generation Investment Management, a firm that encourages companies to operate more sustainably and to strive to not exhaust natural resources. Gore applied journalism to his new business interests. In September of 2001 he used his studies of the corporate world to publish the book *From Red Tape to Results: Creating a Government That Works Better and Costs Less.*

Late in 2002, Gore decided not to run again for public office, the first time in many years. In 1988, at thirty-nine years old, he had vied for the presidency. In 1992 and 1996 he ran with Bill Clinton. Then in 2000 he had made his second presidential run. Gore thought about running again in 2004, but decided to serve the public in different ways.

Gore continued to teach and give speeches. He also wrote books with Tipper about American families. In November of 2002, Henry Holt & Co. published *The Spirit of Family,* which contained 250 photographs of contemporary American families. The book captured the dramatic changes that had taken place in families over the past two generations, as families grew more diverse. In November of 2003, Owl Books published the Gores' second book, *Joined at the Heart: The Transformation of the American Family.* The Gores discussed the social, economic, and cultural changes American families had faced over the last half century.

During this time, while focusing on families, the Gores suffered their own loss. On December 16, 2004, Gore's ninety-two-year-old mother, Pauline, died.

Within five months, Gore had thrown himself back into writing, publishing the book *Common Sense Government*. In it he argued that the U.S. government needs to shift its priorities, and realize that American citizens are its customers, whose needs come first.

That same spring of 2005 Gore gave a power-point presentation on the environment to a gathering in Los Angeles, hosted by environmental activist Laurie David. She suggested, along with another producer, that his presentation be turned into a movie. Eventually, despite his skepticism, the presentation became the basis for the movie *An Inconvenient Truth*. A year later Gore published a book by the same name.

The book and movie led to newfound fame for Gore. "We are now faced with the fact, my friends, that tomorrow is today," Gore wrote, quoting Martin Luther King Jr. "We are confronted with the fierce urgency of now. In this unfolding conundrum of life and history, there is no such thing as being too late."

An Inconvenient Truth was a hit. It grossed about $49 million, making it the third highest-grossing documentary ever. Gore's companion book to the movie was a hit as well, reaching number one on the *New York Times* bestseller list. In 2007, *An Inconvenient Truth* won an Academy Award for best documentary.

Gore donated all the proceeds from the book and movie to The Alliance for Climate Protection. Formed by Gore, the Alliance for Climate Protection aims to persuade people around the world of the urgency of adopting solutions for

Gore attends a screening of *An Inconvenient Truth,* a documentary based on his book. *(Courtesy of AP Images/Elise Amendola)*

the climate crisis. In July of 2007, it sponsored Live Earth, a worldwide concert bringing together more than 2 billion people, across seven continents. More than 150 musicians, ranging from the Red Hot Chili Peppers to Snoop Dogg to Madonna, played for twenty-four hours to raise awareness for environmental causes.

Along with voicing his environmental concerns, Gore also began actively criticizing George W. Bush's domestic and military policies. In May of 2007 he wrote the book, *The Assault on Reason.* Gore evaluated the Bush administration's actions leading up to the terrorist attacks on September 11, 2001, when nineteen terrorists hijacked four planes and flew two planes into the World Trade Centers in New York City and another into the Pentagon outside of Washington. Passengers overwhelmed the hijackers on the fourth plane, crashing it into a field in Pennsylvania before it could reach its intended target. Gore charged that Bush ignored terrorist threats previous to the attack. He also accused Bush of playing on people's fears of another terrorist attack to dishonestly get support for invading Iraq.

Gore further argued that the war, with its lack of international support, made America less safe and isolated the United States. Gore also accused Bush of undermining the constitutional system of check and balances in his efforts to expand executive power.

By the middle of 2007, Americans began to wonder if Al Gore would make his third run for president. He has responded that he has no plans to run for office again. But with Gore arguably more famous, influential, and popular than ever, many wonder if he will reconsider this decision.

Gore's defeat in 2000 did not silence him. Instead, it has sharpened his convictions to speak his mind about the many ways to make a difference. He continues to work diligently to protect and improve the land, the air, and the water that sustains all life on Earth. In or out of politics, Al Gore Jr. will be impacting not just American politics, but the entire world for years to come.

Timeline

1948 Born in Tennessee on March 31.

1965 Graduates from St. Albans School for Boys; meets Mary
Elizabeth "Tipper" Aitcheson; enters Harvard
University.

1969 Graduates from Harvard; enlists in U.S. Army.

1970 Marries Mary Elizabeth "Tipper" Aitcheson on
May 19.

1971 After six months in Vietnam, returns home in June;
begins working as a reporter for the *Tennessean.*

1973 First daughter, Karenna, is born; attends Vanderbilt
University Law School.

1976 Elected to the U.S. House of Representatives.

1977 Second daughter, Kristin, is born.

1978 Reelected to his second term as a congressman.

1979 Third daughter, Sarah, is born.

1980 Elected to a third term.

1982 Son, Albert III, is born; reelected to fourth term.

1983 Sister, Nancy, dies of lung cancer.

1984 Elected to the U.S. Senate.

1987 Announces candidacy for president of the United States.

1988 Withdraws from presidential race after losing the New York primary.

1989 Son, Albert, is hit by a car and severely injured.

1990 Reelected for another term as a U.S. senator.

1992 Book, *Earth in the Balance*, published; Bill Clinton chooses him as his vice presidential running mate; Clinton and Gore elected to office.

1993 Sworn into office on January 20; helps pass NAFTA, creates a plan to streamline government.

1996 Clinton and Gore reelected for a second term; helps pass Telecommunications Act; creates a White House Web site.

1997 Signs the Kyoto Treaty; his book, *Businesslike Government: Lessons Learned from America's Best Companies,* is published.

1998 Clinton administration weathers a scandal; father dies.

1999 Clinton avoids impeachment; announces candidacy for U.S. president.

2000 Wins the Democratic nomination and chooses

Joe Liebermann as a running mate; after a bitterly contested election, concedes to George W. Bush.

2001   Third book, *From Red Tape to Results: Creating a Government That Works Better and Costs Less,* is published.

2002   Decides not to run for president; publishes *The Spirit of Family* and *Joined at the Heart: The Transformation of the American Family* with Tipper.

2004   Mother dies.

2005   Publishes *Common Sense Government*; movie and book *An Inconvenient Truth* released.

2007   Movie wins an Academy Award; publishes *An Assault on Reason;* Americans wonder whether he will run again for president in 2008.

Sources

CHAPTER ONE: Tennessee's Son

p. 13, "There was but . . ." David Maraniss and Ellen Nakashima, *The Prince of Tennessee: Al Gore Meets His Fate* (New York: Simon & Schuster, 2000), 22.

p. 14, "The twang of . . ." Bob Zelnick, *Gore: A Political Life* (Washington, DC: Regnery Publishing, 1999), 13.

p. 14, "I'll ask him . . ." Laura Jeffrey, *Al Gore: Leader for the New Millennium* (Berkeley Heights, NJ: Enslow Publishers, 1999), 14-15.

p. 16, "Love—not the . . ." Bill Turque, *Inventing Al Gore* (New York: Random House, 2001), 38-39.

p. 18, "Al's father would . . ." Ibid., 33.

CHAPTER TWO: Harvard, War, and Love

p. 24, "In September . . ." Turque, *Inventing Al Gore*, 60.

p. 26, "Ours was the class . . ." Zelnick, *Gore: A Political Life*, 49.

p. 26, "If you have . . ." "Conscription in the United States," *Dispatch* (Lexington, NC) *Online*, http://ldedit.us.publicus. com/apps/pbcs.dll/section?category=NEWS&template =wki&text=conscription_in_the_United_States.

p. 26, "In Carthage, Tennessee . . ." Jeffrey, *Al Gore: Leader for the New Millennium*, 23.

p. 26, "His death could . . ." Turque, *Inventing Al Gore,* 63.

p. 27, "Make your choice . . ." Ibid., 68.

CHAPTER THREE: Serving His Country

p. 31, "A lot of guys . . ." Turque, *Inventing Al Gore*, 82.

p. 32, "The men themselves . . ." Zelnick, *Gore: A Political Life*, 68.

p. 35, "I can't imagine . . ." Jeffrey, *Al Gore: Leader for the New Millennium*, 28.

p. 37, "It just came . . ." Ibid., 31-32.

p. 37, "meat and three" Turque, *Inventing Al Gore,* 124.

p. 37, "If I have . . ." Ibid., 117.

p. 38, "My family and . . ." Ibid., 128.

CHAPTER FOUR: Making a Difference

p. 46, "Tomorrow morning . . ." Jeffrey, *Al Gore: Leader for the New Millennium*, 39.

p. 46, "cultural terrorist," Ibid., 40.

p. 47, "I know exactly . . ." Ibid., 42.

CHAPTER FIVE: Hope and Heartache

p. 48, "Should the senator . . ." Turque, *Inventing Al Gore,* 175.

p. 49, "have a single . . . at any level," Jeffrey, *Al Gore: Leader for the New Millennium*, 46.

p. 50, "Smile . . ." Ibid.

p. 50, "Senator Sir . . ." Turque, *Inventing Al Gore,* 203.

p. 54, "It was a . . ." Jeffrey, *Al Gore: Leader for the New Millennium*, 50.

p. 55, "When you've seen . . ." Ibid., 49.

p. 56, "Every time I . . ." Turque, *Inventing Al Gore,* 231-232.

p. 56, "I would like . . ." Jeffrey, *Al Gore: Leader for the New Millennium*, 53.

p. 58, "Read my lips . . . " "George H. W. Bush Acceptance Speech. Republican National Convention, August 18, 1988," George Bush Presidential Library and Museum,

http://bushlibrary.tamu.edu/research/archives.html.

p. 58, "It was a . . ." Ibid., 55.

p. 59, "the most insignificant . . ." Ibid., 57.

p. 60, "most importantly . . ." Ibid., 58.

p. 60, "I could die . . ." Ibid., 57.

p. 60, "Hi Tipper . . ." Ibid., 10.

p. 61-62, "All of us . . ." Ibid., 59.

p. 62-63, "Al and Bill's . . ." Ibid., 60.

p. 63, "You're the most . . ." Ibid., 61.

p. 63, "Our nation found . . ." Ibid., 63-65.

p. 63, "Ozone Man . . ." Ibid., 65.

p. 64, "Gore has written . . ." Ibid., 66.

p. 65, "Both of the . . ." Ibid.

p. 65, "crusading housekeeper," Ibid., 67.

p. 65, "That Gore! . . . " Maraniss and Nakashima, *The Prince of Tennessee: Al Gore Meets His Fate*, 278.

CHAPTER SIX: Inside the White House

p. 68, "A federal worker . . ." Jeffrey, *Al Gore: Leader for the New Millennium*, 71-72.

p. 70, "The Vice President . . ." Ibid., 75.

p. 72, "crazy lady behind . . ." Maraniss and Nakashima, *The Prince of Tennessee: Al Gore Meets His Fate*, 258.

p. 72, "Nice house . . . vice president," Ibid., 262.

p. 73, "Now doesn't it . . ." Jeffrey, *Al Gore: Leader for the New Millennium*, 80.

p. 76, "Don't go down . . ." Ibid., 88.

p. 78, "It was the . . ." Turque, *Inventing Al Gore,* 336.

p. 79, "high crimes and misdemeanors," "The Impeachment Trial," *PBS.org*, http://www.pbs.org/newshour/impeachment/ starr_archive2.html.

p. 80, "Mr. President . . ." Ibid., 350.

CHAPTER SEVEN: A Valiant Battle

p. 83, "You must become . . ." Ibid., 365.

p. 86, "The networks giveth . . ." Elaine Landau, *The 2000 Presidential Election* (New York: Children's Press, 2002), 14.

p. 87, "Circumstances have changed . . . have to do," Jeffrey Toobin, *Too Close to Call* (New York: Random House, 2001), 25.

p. 89, "It's a tricky . . ." Ibid., 13.

p. 90, "Gore Got More . . ." Ibid., 79.

p. 91, "Now that the . . ." Landau, *The 2000 Presidential Election,* 28.

p. 93, "Now the Supreme Court . . ." Ibid., 32-33.

p. 93, "Just moments ago . . ." Toobin, *Too Close to Call,* 269.

p. 93-94, "As for the battle . . ." Maraniss and Nakashima, *The Prince of Tennessee: Al Gore Meets His Fate,* 293-294.

CHAPTER EIGHT: A Call for Change

p. 97, "Hi, I'm . . ." David Remick, "The Wilderness Campaign," *New Yorker,* September 13, 2004.

p. 97, "You know the . . ." Ibid.

p. 98, "Mr. President . . . really won," Ibid.

p. 99, "We are now . . ." Al Gore, *An Inconvenient Truth: The Planetary Emergency of Global Warming and What We Can Do About It* (New York: Rodale, 2006), 10.

Bibliography

Berke, Richard L. "The Gore Guide to the Future." *New York Times Sunday Magazine,* February 22, 1998.

"Conscription in the United States." *Dispatch* (Lexington, NC) *Online,* http://ldedit.us.publicus.com.

Gore, Al. *The Assault on Reason.* New York: Penguin Press, 2007.

————. *An Inconvenient Truth: The Planetary Emergency of Global Warming and What We Can Do About It.* New York: Rodale, 2006.

————. *Earth in the Balance: Ecology and the Human Spirit.* New York: Houghton Mifflin, 1992.

Heilemann, John. "The Comeback Kid." *New York Magazine,* May 22, 2007.

Jeffrey, Laura. *Al Gore: Leader for the New Millennium.* Berkeley Heights, NJ, 1999.

Landau, Elaine. *The 2000 Presidential Election.* New York: Children's Press, 2002.

Maraniss, David, and Ellen Nakashima. "Al Gore, Growing Up in Two Worlds." *Washington Post,* October 10, 1999.

————. *The Prince of Tennessee: Al Gore Meets His Fate.* New York: Simon & Schuster, 2000.

Remnick, David. "The Wilderness Campaign." *New Yorker,* September 13, 2004.

Toobin, Jeffrey. *Too Close to Call.* New York: Random House, 2001.

Turque, Bill. *Inventing Al Gore.* New York: First Mariner Books, 2000.

Zelnick, Bob. *Gore: A Political Life.* Washington, DC: Regnery Publishing, Inc., 1999.

Web sites

http://www.climatecrisis.net
This is the official site for *An Inconvenient Truth,* featuring information about the movie, the science behind global warming, and tips to reduce, reuse, and recycle.

http://clinton4.nara.gov
This Web site provides background information on the Gores and the Clintons during their years in the White House, offering biographies, speeches, a history of the White House, and information about the government's workings.

http://www.algore.org
A "Draft Gore" movement is underway, and this Web site is the place to go to find out more about the all-volunteer, grassroots campaign to draft Al Gore for president in 2008.

Index